◆ BILL KATZ ◆

DONALD'S VANITY TANTRUMS

ILLUSTRATED BY JOE YOUNG

JUBILEE PUBLISHING

JUBILEE PUBLISHING

Text and illustrations © 2020 by Bill Katz

Illustrations by Joe Young. Coloring by Kyle Young and Paige Young

Designed by Lisa Vega

All rights reserved. This book or any portion thereof may not be reproduced or used in any manner whatsoever without the express written permission of the publisher except for the use of brief quotations in a book review. For information address Bill Katz (insert email address or other contact information here)

Printed in the United States of America

First Edition 2020

Second Edition 2023

Third Edition 2024

Fourth Edition 2026

ISBN:978-1-7355825-1-1 (hardcover edition)

ISBN:978-1-7355825-0-4 (paperback edition)

ISBN:978-1-7355825-2-8 (ebook edition)

INTRODUCTION

I began writing about Donald J. Trump the day after his election on November 9, 2016. I was as shocked as were so many of you that a man with such an unstable past, complemented by a lifetime of sleazebag behavior and moral ineptitude, a man of congenital mendacious qualities who made a career out of gaming the system, our government and anyone foolish enough to engage him in business dealings — was now going to be our president.

I didn't set out to write a book. But there was something about Donald Trump that held my interest. In the early 1990s, he came to my hometown of Hartford, Connecticut because he wanted to build a casino. But the Mohegans (and later the Mashantucket Pequots), both Native Connecticut tribes, were already hammering out an exclusive deal with our then governor, Lowell P. Weicker, and our mayor, Carrie Saxon Perry, who played an ancillary role, to give exclusive gambling rights to the tribe in exchange for the state receiving 25% of the revenue from the slot machines. To which Trump replied, "They don't look like Indians to me."

That was so long ago, during a time when Trump was only a crook, a tax cheat and a liar. Now the Trump Animal House, alternately known as the White House and all of the shenanigans taking place inside, has come to pass. My notes began the day after Trump was elected and continued through the fall of 2019. I've included a few more scribbles from 2020. I've run out of gas.

We are experiencing the Covid-19 virus pandemic in the 21st century. When I was a child, my mother, Rose, recounted her childhood experience with the Influenza of 1918 when Woodrow Wilson was president. She lived through dreadful and frightening times. She spoke of the large numbers of dead – some people were tagged as dead even though they were still alive. Fortunately they didn't have the ineptitude of Trump to turn it into a political mess.

I try to write with an eye toward the humorous side of life. I admired columnist Art Buchwald during his tenure at the Washington Post, and the iconic American humorist, Mark Twain. As a student at Hartford Public High School in Connecticut, I occasionally snuck out the side door at lunchtime and with my bag in hand, walked to the nearby Mark Twain House and sat on the porch to eat my sandwich and apple. I fantasized that Twain would come out his door to say "hello." Then I would converse with him about some important matters of the day – maybe President Nixon. After which, I would say goodbye and dutifully return to school.

The short pieces herein take the form of satires, spoofs and commentaries. Some are a combination of fiction and events, not unlike our Commander-in-Grief.

They are not in chronological order so don't get upset. As Frank Sinatra sang, "I did it my way."

The fictional stories include a character posing as Trump's only longtime friend, Bobo the Clown. Bobo comes to life in the early morning hours to keep Trump company and to write and co-write many of his tweets. After developing this character in a few of my pieces, I realized that I had borrowed from Buchwald's creation of Bonzo in the White House during the Reagan administration. I tip my hat to Art and carry on in his spirit. "Bobo" in Portuguese signifies an idiot or a fool: *fazer de bobo*.

This book is among many to denigrate Donald Trump. If we can laugh about it, maybe the trauma we have collectively experienced during this god-forsaken era will diminish. Our wounded spirits will heal.

The air is now escaping from this balloon. Even Trump's hair weave is starting to look ratty. You know what they say: "Hair today, gone tomorrow."

ACKNOWLEDGMENTS

Some of the good folks who gave me advice want to remain anonymous, because of the political nature of the subject. My first editor works for both conservatives and liberals. My friend and neighbor, Alyssa Peterson, helped with editing, formatting and fixing my computer on numerous occasions. Another friend John Simmons, former professor of Biology from Trinity College in Hartford (and now deceased), helped me with proofing and editing. And so has my final editor, Anne Sheffield, who kindly allowed me to weed her extensive wild garden while weeding my words and improving my content. And not forgetting Lisa Vega for her creative design work.

I thank Joe Young and his son and daughter, Kyle and Paige, for providing illustrations. Dennis Kaplan, professor of English at Bay Path University in East Longmeadow, Massachusetts, happily assisted me and collaborated on a few stories.

Dennis is a kindred spirit kind of friend. We first encountered each other in the Hartford Courant newspaper comments sections. Dennis and I were the lefties who battled the population of right-wing posters. We bounced off of each other. Days before the newspaper closed the public comments (we were proving to be uncontrollable with our comments and often complained to the editors and publisher,) I reached out to him to make contact just in the nick of time.

When I met Dennis in person, he encouraged me to write about Trump and then discouraged me at the same time. He never found Trump funny, and thought trying to make Trump funny would be a waste of time. But I want to dedicate this book to him because after all, he was inspirational. But our friendship was short lived. Dennis passed from this life in June, 2020.

As Dennis wrote, "The problem with lampooning Trump, especially when using satire, is that Trump is already so absurd, so ready to do any fucken thing, it makes it almost impossible to caricature him and his doings. But good luck trying. I've taken to ignoring the whole freakin' thing in order to stay at least somewhat sane as we steadily become a bizzaro world of drooling idiots. And that's the simple truth, Ruth."

Last but not least, I want to thank my friend Cynthia Bulaong (director of Artist's Open Studio Hartford) for patiently listening to me crab about additions and making frequent last minute changes while remaining on this continuous journey to expose the monster in the White House.

I thank everyone who is mentioned here and those who are not.

DONALD'S VANITY TANTRUMS

TABLE OF CONTENTS

1. Introduction..III
2. Acknowledgments..VII
3. First Press Conference of the Incoming President........................1
4. Bobo and Donald: Two Fictional Characters...............................3
5. U.S. Sen. Mitch McConnell on the Impeachment Process.............5
6. Phone Conversation Between Trump and Mexican President Enrique Pena...7
7. Reverse Presidential Evolution...9
8. The New Washington Graduate School of Disgusting American Politics..11
9. Where Has Trump Gone..13
10. Evacuation Plans for Washingtonians.....................................17
11. An Ode to Would-be President Hillary Clinton........................19
12. Nixon Versus Trump: Trump's Narcissistic Personality Disorder.....21
13. Not So Fake Late Breaking News Bulletin..............................25
14. Welcome to the New Snazzy Nazi States of America.................27
15. Trump Word Usage..29
16. A Fable: Coming to Amerigus; Terra Nova do Bacalhau..............31
17. Trump's Counseling Session with His Old Friend, Bobo.............33
18. Trump Club at the Great Gatsby..35
19. Talking Points Used By the Trump Administration...................37
20. Donny's First Trick or Treat at the White House......................39
21. "He Knew What He Signed Up For." (Trump to the Widow of Sgt. La David Johnson)..43
22. Thanksgiving Turkeys Pardoned..45
23. Future Memoirs of the Trump era...47
24. New White House Wall...51
25. Mueller Interviews Trump..55

26. A Fireside Chat 57
27. Was it a Good Week for Trump? Ah . . . No............................ 59
28. Another Early Morning Chat with Bobo................................. 61
29. Rex Tillerson is Fired and a Bunch More Stuff........................ 63
30. It's a Dark and Stormy Night 65
31. Beam Me Up, Scotty: Scott Pruitt's New Agency for Holistic Standards Through Unobstructed Pollution 67
32. Environmental Protection Agency 69
33. Trump Meets Kim Jong-un.. 71
34. Trump Goes to Bed with a Cheeseburger 73
35. Moe, Larry, Curly and Rudy... 75
36. Trump is Clean as a Toilet Handle.. 77
37. Another Press Conference... 79
38. George Herbert Walker Bush's Letter to Incoming Bill Clinton 81
39. Another 'Trick or Treat' at the White House 83
40. State of the Union Address.. 87
41. A Swanky Suite in a Five Red Star Hanoi Hotel...................... 89
42. "Nobody Disobeys My Orders Including the Easter Bunny" 93
43. What Some Ancient Rulers Have in Common with Trump........... 95
44. Mockumentary Mini Series.. 97
45. Why are We Screaming at Each Other? 99
46. Testimonials Against Joe Biden.. 101
47. Falling into the Wrong Arms 103
48. Trouble in the Wee Hours... 105
49. Ladies and Gentlemen, the 46th President of the United States..... 107
50. A Coup D'etat To Make America Great Again 109
51. This Convention of Criminals and Clowns 111
52. Is it Over? 113

53. Symbolic Patricide of Don Junior 115
54. The Women's March on Washington 117
55. My Cat Babe and Donald Trump 121
56. Fred Jackson and the Second American Revolution 123
57. The Citizen Kane Movie of Tomorrow: Citizen Trump.................... 129
58. Donald Confesses His Sins 131
59. From the Office of Truth Social: Donald Trump............................ 133
60. The Fricken Disaster Which is Trump and Project 2025 135
61. The Medium is the Message 137
62. "They're Eating Cats & Dogs Says J.D. Vance"............................... 139
63. The Emperor Has No Clothes 141
64. Ghislaine Maxwell: "Trump Told Me Not to Bring Him Any Girls Older Than 14" 143
65. The Nightmare that has Become Reality...................................... 145
66. State's Rights: Stopping Deployment of Federal Troops 147
67. Blue Daze.. 149
68. Tragedy at the White House 151
69. James Comey, Hillary Clinton and I need a Double Shot of Whiskey... 153
70. 'Twaz The Night Before … Oppsie Daisy - What Was It? 157
71. From the Offices of the Greenland Noble Peace Committee........... 159
72. About the Author 161

FIRST PRESS CONFERENCE OF THE INCOMING PRESIDENT

The Golden Shower Caper

"It's a lie . . . It's fake news . . . It's a total political witch-hunt."

Wednesday, Jan. 11, 2017, I had just finished supper and I had tapped the TV zapper to the public television channel just in time to hear, no. . . No it couldn't be something about . . . No it couldn't be. But it was. President-elect Donald Trump in front of a phalanx of American flags in the lobby of Trump Tower.

BuzzFeed was outing Trump's alleged hotel peccadilloes in Moscow and Trump was refusing to let BuzzFeed ask questions at the press conference by repeatedly calling the reports "Fake news. It's a total political witch-hunt."

This was the incoming president's first news conference? My

attention was naturally aroused. What could possibly have happened? Since uncorroborated news stories are usually not published by the mainstream media, I had to search online for the full story.

BuzzFeed has rapidly become mainstream and is partially owned by NBC Universal. The whispers were that President-elect Trump paid Russian prostitutes in Moscow to urinate on his hotel bed in the president's suite – the same one that President Barack Obama slept in. But was Trump in bed when the alleged peeing occurred? Anyone can hire someone to pee on a bed. But not everyone enjoys lounging underneath a golden shower.

The U.S. director of National Intelligence, James Clapper, denied leaking claims that Russia possessed compromising personal and financial information on Trump. At the same time, Clapper tendered his resignation.

Some call this Trumpian erotica "Pissgate." Getting peed on in the wrong place lowers expectations of the most powerful man on earth.

The suffix "gate" was added to scandals after Richard Nixon's "Watergate" crisis. Insider knowledge is an advantage in any reelection campaign. So it was with Russian operatives gaining online access to Hillary Clinton's emails.

Trump has a fascination with gold, whether it's the color or actual gold, or just the word. But Trump is gemaphobic, as he said in an obvious reference to the accusations of the golden shower capers. But urine is an astringent. So why would our incoming president suggest that he would never submit to a "golden shower"?

Emperor Caligula hasn't anything on this president!

"*Laissez les bon temps roulez*," as they say in New Orleans. "Let the good times roll."

BOBO AND DONALD: TWO FICTIONAL CHARACTERS

Since the president-elect began tweeting in the early hours of the morning, he has posted pretty outrageous stuff. But what the general public doesn't realize is that Trump has owned a clown doll from childhood named Bobo. And Bobo has quite an independent streak and awakens when everyone else is snoozing. He then logs on to his master's computer desk and begins tweeting. Later, when Trump arises, he is flooded with all kinds of questions and criticisms about the asinine remarks he supposedly tweeted earlier.

Like the other morning, Bobo tweeted "Anyone who burns the American flag should lose citizenship."

Trump: "Bobo, now what did you tweet?"

Bobo: "Donny, I'm just trying to make sure the alt-right stays strong and on point."

Trump: "You said that Bobo? It's illegal. Oh man, that's tremendous."

Bobo: "Donny, can I be your press spokes doll?"

"No Bobo," said Trump," Katrina Pierson has that job now. You're beginning to make a monkey out of me."

"Can I be Secretary of Defense? Please, please?"

"No, I chose Marine General "Mad Dog" Mattis for the job. Get out of here, Bobo. I'm sorry. I'm a 70-year-old grandfather and you're making me look like a 13-year-old teen posting all that crap. We have been together for a long time. Look Bobo, only you and me will know who is really tweeting during my administration. After I leave office, I'll write my "tell-all" memoirs and we'll call it, "Those Wonderful Years of President Trump and Bobo the Clown. It will be a fabulous book. Nothing like it ever before."

Bobo: "I don't want to be known as a clown, Donny,"

"OK," President-elect Trump responded. "Then I'll be the clown. Ok Bobo? You can be one of my advisors."

U.S. SEN. MITCH MCCONNELL ON THE IMPEACHMENT PROCESS

McConnell on Clinton Impeachment, Feb. 12, 1998
"Our nation is indeed at a crossroads. We will pursue the search for truth, or we will dodge, weave and evade the truth? I am of course referring to the investigation into serious allegations of illegal conduct by the president of the United States – that the president has engaged in a persistent pattern and practice of obstruction of justice. The allegations are grave, the investigation is legitimate, and ascertaining the truth, the whole truth and nothing but the unqualified, unevasive truth is absolutely critical."

McConnell on the Trump Impeachment, Dec. 12, 2019
"Everything I do during this (trial), I'm coordinating with the White House counsel. There will be no difference between the president's position and our position as to how to handle this to the extent that we can. Exactly how we go forward I'm going to coordinate with the president's lawyers, so there won't be any difference between us on how to do this.

I'm going to take my cues from the president's lawyers."

PHONE CONVERSATION BETWEEN TRUMP AND MEXICAN PRESIDENT ENRIQUE PENA NIETO

January 27, 2017

A phone call comes in to the White House and is sent to the president's office.

Trump: "President Niento, Donald Trump here."

Niento: "Bueno. Presidente Trump, que dia es convenience para mi visita a Washington?"

Trump: "Cut the shit, Enrique. I know you speak English. We

	are meeting next month. How much is Mexico kicking in for the wall? We need border control."
Nieto:	"Senior Pendejo, I am not giving one peso for that wall. Shouldn't we talk about NAFTA instead?"
Trump:	"Nieto, I'm planning on building a big wall – the biggest wall ever. I will charge 20 percent tariffs on all Mexican imports until the wall is finished. As for NAFTA, you can send that agreement down the shithole Rio Grande. And I know what pendejo means. It means a president that uses his pen to sign executive orders."
Niento:	"Presidente Pendejo, I've got better things to do besides listening to a half-baked potato like you. Our meeting is canceled. Say hola to the family."

REVERSE PRESIDENTIAL EVOLUTION

April 22, 2019

"I hope I shall possess firmness and virtue enough to maintain what I consider the most enviable of all titles, the character of an honest man."—*George Washington*

"You can fool all the people some of the time, and some of the people all the time, but you cannot fool all the people all the time."—*Abraham Lincoln*

"Ask not what your country can do for you, but what you can do for your country."—*John Fitzgerald Kennedy*

"Now, as a nation, we don't promise equal outcomes, but we were founded on the idea everybody should have an equal opportunity to succeed. No matter who you are, what you look like, where you come from, you can make it. That's the essential promise of America. Where you start should not determine where you end up."—*Barack Obama*

"Statements are made about me by certain people in the crazy Mueller Report, in itself written by 18 angry Democrat Trump haters which are fabricated and... total bullshit."—*Donald Trump*

THE NEW WASHINGTON GRADUATE SCHOOL OF DISGUSTING AMERICAN POLITICS

An exchange between the Registrar's office and
a prospective Saudi graduate student

"Registrar, may I help you?"

"I'm interested in your course schedule for the new semester. I understand you offer both master's and Ph.D. programs."

"Are you an American citizen by birth?"

"What difference should that make?"

"Because these student spots are in demand and foreign students get confused when they begin their core studies on American sleaze, government dysfunction, and the need to use money for its intended purpose: to fully corrupt congressmen and senators. We even have a street here in town that facilitates this corruption, K Street. Foreign students become confused and usually drop out before graduation. We seek motivated students who will fully participate in the American system of immoral and unethical behavior. We now have internship programs at the executive level in the White House where you can get hands-on experience."

"How do I apply?"

"Have you corrupted or otherwise seduced anyone in government yet? Have you filed for bankruptcy? Have you swindled anyone lately? Those are the criteria we use in determining which promising students to accept."

"I'm a Saudi citizen."

"Oh terrific! We understand you people are decapitation specialists. Would you be interested in our work/study program at the White House?"

WHERE HAS TRUMP GONE?

A White House Press Conference

Reporter:	Something is going on in the White House. Secret Service agents ran past me in the hallway and now are on the rooftop with telescopic rifles.
Sarah Huckabee Sanders:	No, nothing's going on today. Ya, nothing, not really.
CNN Staff Writer:	I overheard coming in that the president has departed. Can you elaborate please?

Sanders:	We are just not in face-to-face contact with him this morning. We are fine. The nation is secure. I can tell you that.

(Chief of Staff Mick Mulvaney peeps his head in the door)

Mulvaney:	Hi folks. Uh Sarah, I'm gonna take over this meeting. I will introduce all of you to a few cabinet members in a moment. There is no need to panic. President Trump has indeed disappeared for the moment. But we know he is still here, in a way.

(Vice President, Secretary of State and several cabinet secretaries enter the room)

Mulvaney:	I'd like to introduce Acting Secretary of Defense Patrick Shanahan. The military is on full alert. We've withdrawn some troops from the Mexican border and brought them to Washington where they have more important duties. But there is no need to panic, as Mike said earlier. We just can't seem to locate him. He's tweeting now? Who said that?
Sec'y of Commerce Wilbur Ross:	We got him. Everything is fine. The president has been tweeting all morning long.
WH Reporter:	Then who's in charge?

Pence: Ladies and Gentlemen, until president Trump is found, the Constitution says that I'm in charge here. Please open your Twitter feed. The president is now tweeting.

Trump: As your best leader in the history of the United States, I am fine. I've decided to go to Twitterland. This place has a wall around the whole city, financed without having to shut down the government of the city-state. I'm happy here. Bobo the Clown is with me as my longtime faithful friend. I intend to continue as president, but not in body. I can no longer live in that small White House. Please tell Melania I'm not bringing her here. I've found a new love in Twitterland, Stormy Daniels.

EVACUATION PLANS FOR WASHINGTONIANS

December 4, 2017

There has been some chatter in online talk rooms (and in real life) about a scenario in which Premier Kim Jung Un of North Korea is planning to launch an atomic bomb at Washington. My cousin Barney, his wife Jennifer and kids live in D.C. and he told me that some residents are already doing dry runs to Barrackville, West Virginia, and other nearby towns to purchase houses. Barney has a small art gallery in Georgetown and he is concerned that if the bomb comes, his paintings will become radioactive. Art dealers are like that. They don't think first of the human cost. It's always the paintings. I know because I am an art dealer.

Trump is feeling the heat of investigations regarding his continual abuse of power. Now the House of Representatives is investigating the president for withholding Congressional military funding for Ukraine in order to investigate his Democratic political rival, Joe Biden and his son, Hunter. Many high-ranking officials are being investigated and a few of them are already serving their country in federal prisons. It's not that far-fetched that Trump could start a war in order to deflect attention away from his impeachable offenses.

Trump has the perfect psychological profile to start one. Any number of hot spots, such as Iran or North Korea, provides the perfect context to attack their growing nuclear capability. This makes Washingtonians nervous. On one of the drives Barney and his family have made to Barrackville, they stopped by a farmer's house to ask about homes for sale.

The farmer came out holding a shotgun.

"What do you want here?"

"I'm looking to buy a house. Do you know of any for sale?"

"Git off my property."

"I was only asking about a house."

"You have 30 seconds to git off my property."

Poor Barney ran back to his car and sped off with Jen and didn't stop until they reached Washington.

"Honey," said Jennifer, "It's still safer living there than in D.C. with that mad man in the White House. Let's go back to Barrackville next weekend and find a realtor."

AN ODE TO WOULD-BE PRESIDENT HILLARY CLINTON

How Things Might Have Been on Her Watch

The phone rings at the White House switchboard at 3 a.m.

Operator:	White House, who's calling please?
Caller:	The red fox trots quietly at midnight.
Operator:	Ummm, OK, can you hold a moment? (Operator quickly reaches into the bottom desk drawer, grabs her CIA-issued code book and begins flipping pages . . .) Thank you for holding, was that 'The red fox trots quietly at midnight?'
Caller:	Yes.

(The caller is put on hold again while the switchboard operator connects to the North Lawn Secret Service line. Agent Butler, a convenient name for someone stuck on the midnight shift as a glorified administrative assistant, picks up and receives a quick briefing.)

Agent Butler:	Mrs. President? You've just received a coded call through the switchboard. Were you asleep?

Mrs. President:	No Butler, I was just going over some briefs and no, not my husband's.
Agent Butler:	The caller relayed that the 'The red fox trots quietly at midnight.' Do you understand?
Mrs. President:	Uhhhh, no. I'm busy with the nation's business. Let me ask my husband, 'Bill, wake up.'
Former President:	(Yawning deeply) What is it, Hillary?
Mrs. President:	The switchboard has a coded call holding: the caller stated 'The red fox trots quietly at midnight.' Sounds like code from the 90's.
Former President:	Hillary, that doesn't mean anything. It's probably a crank call. Give Agent Butler the new code book. I'm going back to sleep . . .

The White House bedroom light stays on until dawn and all remains secure . . . at least for another day.

NIXON VERSUS TRUMP: CAN WE TALK — TRUMP'S NARCISSISTIC PERSONALITY DISORDER

January 27, 2017

Not since the "Plumbers" from the "Tricky Dick" Nixon administration has such a motley crew been connected to a White House administration as this one. Back then, the crew was hired by Nixon underlings to investigate leaks within the administration and in particular, Daniel Ellsberg's "Pentagon Papers" exposing lies associated with the Vietnam War. With such a smart snoop group assembled, their activities shifted to spying on the Democratic Party headquarters. Their plan was to gain an informational advantage leading up to the reelection of Nixon in 1972.

The "Plumbers" were caught red-handed, arrested and sent to prison. The investigation slowly led up the chain of command until, like the paw prints of a wet dog, stopped at the desk of Nixon himself. Since Tricky Dick had a penchant for secretly taping all of his conversations, one of them implicated him in the break-in. Before the tape was sequestered by Special Prosecutor Archibald Cox, Nixon allegedly had his secretary erase 18 1/2 minutes of possibly incriminating conversation. Nixon resigned before he was impeached by Congress.

It's unfair to compare Nixon to Trump because Nixon was so much more capable as a leader. But I will. Nixon was a skilled politician and wise in the world of international relations. In the end, Nixon's paranoia led him to imagine enemies closing in on him. Trump, on the other hand, has a more diffused and debilitating mental illness. He appears to have a narcissistic sociopathic personality disorder with a dash of psychosis and paranoia.

On his second day in office, Trump disputed the numbers of people who came to the Mall to watch him be sworn into office. His press spokesman, Sean Spicer, gave a briefing insisting that the numbers were greater than Obama's in 2009. This contradicted National Parks Services Director Michael Reynolds's office photos showing much lower numbers. This is huge because he always has to have the biggest, the best, and the most of everything which causes Trump to have vanity tantrums.

Deputy Press Secretary, Sarah Huckabee Sanders, questioned why someone in National Parks shared a tweet in which photos of Trump's inauguration were compared with Obama's inaugural photos from 2009. Oops.

Trump demanded to talk with Reynolds. The White House called his office and for security reasons, had Reynolds call back using a special number.

Reynolds: "Hello, is this the White House?"

"Just a moment, the next voice you hear will be President Trump."

"Reynolds, why the hell are you using fake photos? You know more people attended my inauguration than ever before in the history of the country."

"Yes, Mr. President. Our printer was running low on ink and didn't show all of your supporters at the rear of the Mall."

"And who gave the OK to use a tweet to show these photos? You know I'm the only one in the government who should use Twitter."

According to The New York Times story dated Jan. 26, 2017 (written by Michael D. Shear and Maggie Haberman), "Ms. Sanders said Mr. Trump's decision to call Mr. Reynolds is a reflection of what his supporters find appealing: his willingness to do something himself when he thinks it needs to be done."

NOT SO FAKE LATE BREAKING NEWS BULLETINS

February 1, 2017

LATE BREAKING NEWS BULLETIN

President Trump on Friday, January 28 at 4:42 p.m., suspended entry of all refugees entering the United States for 120 days. The countries included Iran, Iraq, Libya, Somalia, Sudan, Syria, and Yemen.

LATE BREAKING NEWS BULLETIN

Protests have broken out at international airports across the country. Muslim nationals who boarded planes before the ban were taken into custody upon arrival at U.S. airports.

LATE BREAKING NEWS BULLETIN

Acting Attorney General Sally Q. Yates was fired by President Trump after she refused to enforce his executive order. In her opinion, the order closing the nation's borders to refugees and people from predominately Muslim countries was legally indefensible.

LATE BREAKING NEWS BULLETIN

National Security Advisor Mike Flynn said on Wednesday that the Trump administration is putting Iran "on notice" after it tested a ballistic missile.

LATE BREAKING NEWS BULLETIN

A new executive order signed by Trump authorizes the removal of the Statue of Liberty and to send her back to France.

WELCOME TO THE NEW SNAZZY NAZI STATES OF AMERICA

Introducing *The Goose-Step, Two-Step March*
February 25, 2017

A new dance craze is sweeping the nation called, *The Goose-Step, Two-step March*. This invigorating new exercise is easy to learn! First, link arms on the dance floor. As you move backward in line, turn your head to the right and lift your left leg straight up as high as it will go. Then step forward as you turn your head to the left and lift your right leg straight up in the air.

It's very similar to square dancing or line dancing. Soon the dance floor will be filled with goose-steppers. Forward, backward, round and round. If you step out of line, you are tagged, the caller detains you, interrogates you, strip searches you, and sends you off to detainment camps for disloyalty.

This new dance craze is not to be confused with serious charges of criminal activity. By the time the youngins reach the age of reason, they will be quick to form into lines upon request for impromptu *Goose-Step, Two-Step Marches* and other forms of family entertainment.

TRUMP WORD USAGE

December 22, 2017

Comedian George Carlin said there are seven words that could never be spoken (or sung) or hummed on TV. The words related to the human body and body waste. (Included were two extra words that have nothing to do with body parts or bodily waste.) Now, there is a new set of banned words.

Today, Trump has his own forbidden seven words excluded from the lexicon in the Centers for Disease Control in Atlanta. I caution readers who are sensitive to hearing or reading harsh words, so use discretion when viewing them. Here they are: *Vulnerable, Entitlement, Diversity, Transgender, Fetus, Evidence-based, and Science-based.*

For a Trump administration basing its Tweeter releases (the current alternative to press releases) on a constant diatribe of untruths, *Evidence-based* and *Science-based* are a natural anathema to his vocabulary.

Did he ban *Fetus* fearful that researchers might examine the lawful moment when a fetus becomes a person? Some believe a person exists at that sparkling moment when sperm-meets-egg, therefore there is no fetus.

As a populist, Trump's response to world cultures is that *Diversity* is the enemy of White Supremacy, as well as a probable reaction to our former African-American president.

In the World According to Trump, there is no *Entitlement* for anyone except of course, himself. And in the Trump universe, being *Vulnerable* is a loser's bet.

A FABLE: COMING TO AMERIGUS; TERRA NOVA DO BACALHAU

March 8, 2017

(This fable is dedicated to Dr. Ben Carson, Secretary of Housing and Urban Development, who gave this speech to his employees.)

"There were other immigrants who came here in the bottom of slave ships, worked even longer, even harder for less. But they too, had a dream, that one day their sons, daughters, grandsons, great granddaughters, great grandsons, might pursue prosperity and happiness in this land.

"And do you know of all the nations of the world, this one, the United States of America, is the only one big enough and great enough to allow all those people to realize their dream. And this is our opportunity to enhance that dream."

(After reading this remark I realized that being highly educated is no insurance against speaking and believing the most incredible foolhardy notions.)

Once upon a time, in the 17th century, there lived in the lands of Senegambia, on the west coast of Africa, Babba Sanghor and his wife Binata and their two young children. They were a happy family. Their children played with the other children in the Communal Hut of Education in the village square. It was a time filled with laughter and festivities for all.

Babba and Binata would rise every morning to the Sun God of the new day. Babba was a planter of food crops and after sharing java with his loving wife, would go out in his fields along with other villagers to tend crops to sell in the marketplace.

One day, Babba had the extraordinary idea to take his family on vacation. He had heard rumors that Portuguese-owned ships were bringing families from other villages to the far shores of a place called Terra Nova do Bacalhau or New Land of the Codfish. Babba decided to give his family a new experience they would never forget. The trip could be made for little or no cost, so Babba thought. He was excited at the prospect of taking his family to gaze on fare away lands where the mythical great buffalo roamed. He had heard that exotic natives performed dances for visiting tourists.

Babba's family was excited about the prospect of getting away from the daily grind of long days in the fields. His children dreamt at night about visiting to what some called, "The New World." The family packed and organized for a one month visit to this wonderland and a chance to meet people with different customs.

When the departure day arrived, Babba, Binata and their two children bundled off to the ocean shore to await the ships that would take them on the most spectacular journey of their lives.

The End.

And it was the end.

TRUMP'S COUNSELING SESSION WITH HIS OLD FRIEND, BOBO

"Bobo, I'm so sorry I chose Jeff Bouregard Sessions as my attorney general. He won't do anything I tell him to do. He won't fire Rod Rosenstein. He won't fire Robert Mueller. What good is he, Bobo? They're all gonna ruin me."

"Donny, screw them all. You can fire them and pardon yourself. Don't forget that. You have awesome powers as president and no one can stop you."

"Cheeses, Bobo, do you think? Hmm . . . You know you're right."

"Donny, go to Singapore and make Kim Jung-Un eat out of your hand. You are more unpredictable than he is. You scare him, Donny. You know how to scare everybody. And that's why I like you."

"Bobo, I want you to tweet that Trudeau and his Canadians are wussy socialists. Say that he stabbed us in the back. I'll have Bolton say that we got rid of Muammar Gaddafi as a warning to Little Rocket Man."

"We're gonna make America great again, one way or another!

"Donny, can I go to Singapore with you and meet Kim Jung-Un?"

"No Bobo, you might really scare him."

TRUMP CLUB AT THE GREAT GATSBY

July 4, 2017

"Holy Moly," says Richard DeAgazio, a paying guest at Mar-a-Lago, Trump's amusement park for his wealthy patrons.

The Trump entourage huddles over a computer using cell phones to light up the darkened room.

"Wow . . . the center of attention," writes Mr. DeAgazio on his Facebook page as he observes from across the room

The next morning in the White House at 3 a.m., the president is pacing around with Bobo, who instigates posts on Trump's Twitter page.

"Bobo, you should have seen the hullabaloo during dinner with the Jap prime minister."

"Donny, you shouldn't call Shinzo Abe 'the Jap.' That's not nice."

"Whatever, Bobo. Hey, yesterday was a night to remember. Something right out of The Great Gatsby, only greater. We are in charge now, and our rule cannot not be questioned."

"Bobo, I will have to replace that Black guy who carries the nuclear "football" codes in a briefcase. He allowed himself to be photographede with one of my Mar-a-Lago members."

"What is his job, Donny?"

"In case I need to attack some bad hombres while traveling. He has the codes to unlock the suitcase so I can activate a nuclear attack. And it's gonna happen, Bobo, mark my words. It's gonna happen."

"Donny, can I carry the suitcase? I promise to be careful. I won't allow myself to get photographed."

"No, Bobo, I know I could trust you. But the Democrats would accuse me again of playing around with the security of our government. Hey, I'll bet I can increase yearly dues at Mar-a-Lago from $200,000 to $400,000 after last night's evening."

"It's beginning to pay off, Bobo. Just like we knew it would."

TALKING POINTS USED BY THE TRUMP ADMINISTRATION

1. "Don't believe the garbage you read:" (One of Trump's favorite lines.)

2. "It's fake news. It's phony stuff. It didn't happen." (Spoken at Trump's first press conference as president-elect and reiterated thousands of times to brainwash the crowd.)

3. "This is my real hair." (What was not mentioned: his doctor reported that Trump uses Propecia, which is a hair growth stimulant that has a nasty side effect of curtailing the user's ability to become sexually aroused.)

4. "I assure you it's true." (Indicating that which he means is not true.)

5. "We're gonna make America so great again." (Early use of the motto on Feb.10, 2016, after his victory in the New Hampshire primary)

6. "We are gonna bring back jobs. Trust me." (The jobless rate passes that of the Great Recession and now equals the Great Depression.)

7. "We're gonna build a high wall and Mexico will pay for it." (Millions were taken from the Defense budget to pay for it.)

8. "The news media is our enemy" (A sentiment only acceptable in autocratic societies and dictatorships)

9. "Total Baloney." (When Reince Priebus was asked during the week of Feb.20, 2017 if contact had been made between Trump staff and Russian officials, he responded by slandering sandwich meat.)

DONNY'S FIRST TRICK-OR-TREAT AT THE WHITE HOUSE

November 1, 2017

At 5 p.m., as *Trick-or-Treaters* arrive, Secret Service agents pat down each costumed walk-in. This screening continues as Trump and his 3rd wife, First Lady Melania Trump, walk onto the portico laden with sacks of candy.

"Trick-or-treat!" The first spooky ghost slowly walks up to Trump.

Trump: "Melania, they're already here. Don't these people eat dinner?

Melania: "Oh look, Donald, at the little devil. 'Here's some Fireballs.' Honey, he looks familiar."

Trump: "You are dressed as someone who claims he used to work here, but I don't remember any of them. Anyways, he's a little liar. 'Melania, give him some Pay Day candy.' OK, next?"

Papadopulas: "I want more, Mr. President. Boo. Or else. If you give me the keys to the candy warehouse and promise me a pardon, I won't talk anymore."

Trump to Security:	"Get him outta here. Next."
Trump:	"Now who are you, little guy? You have a Manafort face like a plastic toy. How much do you want? All of it? How about some tootsie rolls? We have a tractor full of 'em along with Snickers, out back."
Manafort:	"Mr. President, forget the candy. Just gimme my passport and a flight to Moscow. OK, Mr. President?"
Trump to Security:	"Put him in my Batmobile to Russia with top security clearance. Next?"

"Trick-or-Treat."

Trump:	"What would you like? Is that you, Michael Flynn, under that Halloween mask?"
Flynn:	"Shush, Mr. President. I only need one treat. I was your loyal servant. A ghost told me your private plane is leaving for Moscow later tonight and I need to get onboard."
Trump:	"No problem. Give him some Hershey Kisses, Melania. Next?"

"Trick-or-treat."

Trump:	"You're too old to be trick or treating. The ghost of Halloween past! John Dean III? What are you doing here?"

Dean:	"Mr. President, I testified against Nixon in 1974 and he resigned. My advice is to resign while you can."
Trump:	"Hey, you're scaring the bejesus out of me. Where is Scaramucci? He was named for Halloween. Why isn't Anthony Scaramucci here scaring us?"
Melania:	"Donald, look! It's Steve Bannon dressed as Adolf Hitler!"
Trump:	"Do you want some incendiary devices to drop off at Democratic Party Headquarters? Don't say anything about this."

"Trick-or-Treat"

Trump:	"Oh boy, you're dressed like Robert E. Lee. Cute! Is that you, John Kelly?"
Kelly:	"I want a Three Musketeers bar and a few weeks without controversy."
Trump:	"Melania, just give John what he wants."

"Trick-or-Treat"

Trump:	"Nice Valdimir Putin outfit. Does it have Ivanka's label?"
Putin:	"Da. We have plenty room for you in Russia at Hotel Trump if you need a fast get-away with no fugitive exchange policy."

Trump: "Melania, I'm tired. You? Let's close this thing before someone dresses as Robert Mueller and then I have to fire him. Let's go inside. No more free handouts for these moochers."

"HE KNEW WHAT HE SIGNED UP FOR"

Trump to the Widow of Sgt. La David Johnson
October 20, 2017

The Commander in Chief's duty is to comfort families of deceased soldiers lost in combat. That is, unless the commander is a sociopath incapable of feeling pain for others. This president hasn't the capacity to perform humane gestures.

Sgt. La David Johnson, a Green Beret, was ambushed and killed in an operation in Niger in 2017. When asked to call his widow, Trump said, ". . . he knew what he signed up for. . . but when it happens, it hurts anyway." As Myeshia Johnson related, this made her cry even more; that Trump couldn't remember her husband's name or have it written down.

When U.S. Rep. Frederica Wilson, who represents the district where the fallen soldier's family resides, revealed this story, she was immediately accused of fabricating it. However, Myeshia substantiated Trump's words. How could a president make such an important call and make a widow feel worse? His name is not difficult to say: Sgt. La David Johnson. These fumbling responses are now expected of Trump, given his crude and ignorant behavior. When will those who voted for him regret their vote? Trump will create a tidal wave against his brand of egomaniacal populism. This nation needs a pendulum swing from horrible leadership to a cleansing reaction. Unfortunately, this counter point will come (and has come) at a great cost.

THANKSGIVING TURKEYS PARDONED

November 21, 2017

Upholding the White House tradition, Trump has pardoned two turkeys. However, before this commutation was performed, his inner circle of advisors met to discuss the stunt that included a pardon of human turkeys.

Trump: "Let's get this over with quickly. Kellyanne, I'm afraid that if I touch either of those turkeys while the cameras are rolling, one of them might take a nip out of me. Would that be reason to throw them in the oven?"

Kellyanne Conway: "Mr. President, you can't pardon a turkey and then eat it. Otherwise, it wouldn't be a pardon."

John Kelly:	"We could if it was a military court martial."
Trump:	"How about if we dress up George Papadopulas and Paul Manafort as turkeys. I'll pardon them so they won't talk and the fake media won't know what I did."
Apprentice Contestant Omarosa Manigault:	"My Emperor Trump, don't waste the pardon on those two failed operators. Feed them to the dogs. No, I think you should invite your sons Eric and Donny Jr. over, dress 'em up in turkey costumes, and pardon their asses before Robert Mueller has a chance to subpoena them. Donny Jr. has already said too much in the press about the Russian meetings. If he talks, you're toast. That way, you kill two birds with one stone."
Trump:	"Why would Donny betray me? I disciplined him so he would behave himself. I can't wait to tell the boys what you just said, Omarosa. That's it. I'll pardon my two sons. Throw the turkeys in the oven. I'm getting hungry. Maybe I'll have a cheeseburger while I wait."

FUTURE MEMOIRS OF THE TRUMP ERA

Tell All Book Promotions
December 28, 2017

Omarosa Manigault Newman: *"Memoirs: My Token Black Negrita Days with Donald Trump."*

"Donald J. Trump has been my employer and master for many years. I was his back-up babe and I always had his back. That is, until the latter part of 2017 in the White House. The early months were fun. I could walk into the Oval Office without advance notice and attend meetings with the highest security clearance. I was Trump's go-to-gal.

This all changed when I saw a different side of my leader. I knew Donald had a preference for being around Caucasians, but I never thought I would see the day when my master would openly support white supremacist ideology. My people built this Palace of the People. Now, Chief of Staff John Kelly, who thinks Robert E. Lee was a cool guy, threw this here Negrita out on her ass and disabled my White House pass."

Secretary of State Rex Tillerson: *"Memoirs: My Patriotic Duty in the Trump Administration."*

"When Trump asked me to be the 69th Secretary of State, I was initially proud to serve the nation until I realized the guy was a moron. I had to deny this remark I made but as sure as Texas is the Lone Star

State, I said it and stand by it. He is a moron to the tenth power. The Cabinet considered having clandestine meetings planning the day we would invoke the Twenty Fifth Amendment to wrest control of the government from this psycho-dramatic, demented varmint. I'm not a quitter; Trump fired me before our first meeting.

Steve Bannon: *"Memoirs: Man the Battle Stations, We're Coming for America."*

"I will support Trump unto my dying hour and fight to save America from the terrorist hordes. We have the financing and strategy to enact laws to Make America Great Again. This is a fight to keep the Motherland pure and free of diversity. My brief time in the White House was chaotic, but it restored my faith that we can and will make the White House all White."

Michael Flynn: *"Memoirs: My Short Time Working in the Shadow of Trump."*

"As a retired Lieutenant General from the army, I served the country honorably for 33 years. Then I met Donald Trump who promised me a Rose Garden. Donald said I was a "wonderful man" but later said I was a "liar." I joined the team and yelled "lock her up" referring to Hillary Clinton. I did what the boss told me to do. I became an aide to the Russians. If you think John Deane sang a song to prosecutors back in the Nixon White House, you will understand why I pleaded guilty to lying. I was the inside fall guy and now the American people will know who the real liar is. This may come as a shock to readers, but in my book I detail how Trump was a fully bloomed addlepate. I was railroaded to plead guilty but I'm not guilty if you can believe it."

George Papadopulas: *"Memoirs: I Was Trump's Confidant."*

I pleaded guilty to lying to FBI agents. In exchange, Mueller made me a deal to testify and create back channels with the Russians. I was not "extremely limited" in the Trump campaign as Sarah Huckabee Sanders stated. My book will explain our mission to dig up dirt on Clinton by working with the Russians. Trump sanctioned this interaction."

Paul Manafort: *"Memoirs: Give Me a Break (Letters from a Federal Prison Cell)"*

"I'm not guilty of the crimes for which I have been convicted. I served my president well. And I made a ton of money before and during my brief time in Trump's employ. I have asked the judge to let me bunk with Trump when he is sentenced to prison."

Jeff Sessions: *"Memoirs: My Time as Attorney General."*

"I recused myself from any actions while attorney general because I was paralyzed with fear and felt like a puppet. However, my book will show the ultimate insider's look at a very fragile Trump administration and how events will likely lead to its total collapse."

Anthony Scaramucci: *"Memoirs: Eleven Special Days in the White House"*

"I was appointed communications director and reported directly to Trump. That is until General Kelly became chief of staff and told me I had to ask his permission to meet with the boss going forward. I was quite capable of finding all of the news leakers and firing their asses. I know that Reince Preibus is a freakin paranoid schizophrenic. And Steve Bannon only knows how to pleasure himself. On day 11, John Kelly's Secret Service Storm Troopers escorted me out of the White

House. And that slob Sarah Huckabee Sanders is now the newest ass-kisser press spokesperson at the White House."

John Kelly: *"Memoirs: The Presidential Years Under Trump's Thumb"*

"As a former four-star general, I was trained to be a disciplinarian. The White House was in disarray with political infighting and back-stabbing when I accepted the invitation to become chief of staff. And then, God punished me. I took on this impossible task for the love of my country. For entertainment, the staff leaked embarrassing info on each other. I will for posterity, reveal in detail the inept staff chosen by our Commander-in-Chief, Donald Trump, 45th President of the United States, and soon to be desposed."

Kellyanne Conway: *"Memoirs: The Importance of Expressing Alternative Facts for the Libtards."*

"Working for Trump, my dear friend during the election and later in the White House, has caused this blonde bombshell with brown hair roots to go prematurely gray. I had to use multiple treatments of ultra-blonde hair treatment to achieve the sexy Nordic look required in the White House. It is the White House, after all. Doesn't Donald look sexy as he exits the Oval Office in his long red tie? My polling indicates America will realize that history was on our side. But, my husband George disagrees."

NEW WHITE HOUSE WALL

At a recent Monday morning press briefing

Sarah Huckabee Sanders:	Ah, good morning. The President is initiating a groundbreaking project here in Washington. He has asked for bids to build a high wall around the White House.
CNN's Jim Acosta:	Sarah, I don't understand. The White House already has metal fencing around the whole compound.
Sanders:	Jim, I thought you knew everything around here.
CBS News Correspondent:	Congress has already said 'no' to the Mexican border wall. What is this now?
Sanders:	It's gonna be a tremendous, never before built wall of stone. That's all I can tell you at this time.
Politico Correspondent:	Wait a minute, if this new construction is of stone, the panoramic view of the White House will be lost.

Sanders: What is it that y'all don't understand? (She reads from a script.) The stone will come from an American quarry, not the poor quality materials imported from that shithole country, China. The view will be gone because the President wants to sunbath on the 2nd floor balcony.

BuzzFeed Correspondent: Sarah, what I'm hearing from you, does this wall have anything to do with the wall that Congress wouldn't fund at the Mexican border?

Sanders: No.

ABC News Correspondent: What's wrong with the fencing that's in place now, Sarah?

Sanders: Let me bring out Mick Mulvaney to explain this new White House wall. Your questions are ridiculous and rude and you should be fired.

Mulvaney: As Sarah just announced, this wall will safely enclose the White House grounds for privacy in all matters personal, domestic and foreign. It will be a stone wall. Get it?

NBC Correspondent: Is the White House sending a message that there will be no cooperation with the Mueller Report or the Impeachment hearings?

Mulvaney: What gives you that impression? The President needs a screen erected around the White House to prevent people from knowing what he is doing all day. That's all. This press briefing is over.

MUELLER INTERVIEWS TRUMP

January 9, 2018

Former FBI Director Robert Mueller III, acting as special counsel on the Russian investigation into whether Trump or anyone on his election team colluded with the Russians to receive compromising information on his 2016 opponent, Hillary Clinton:

Mueller: "Mr. President, did you engage in any activity or did any of your staff or volunteers seek any compromising information from Russian operatives?"

Trump: "I'm a very smart man. I'm a genius. I'm smarter than those guys at the Genius Bar at the Apple store. Do you think I would betray my country for an election win over "Lock-Her-Up" Hillary Clinton?

Mueller: "Did you?"

Trump: "I've built hotels all over the world. I've miraculously turned an old U.S. Post Office right down the street from my temporary residence into a Trump hotel. And by the way, I'm turning the White House into an overnight Airbnb for billionaires.

	"There's been no collusion, there's been no crime, and everyone tells me I'm not under investigation. Because honestly, it's very, very bad for our country. It's making our country look foolish."
Mueller:	"Did you or your people or anyone assisting you during the election campaign, seek compromising information about former Secretary of State Hillary Clinton?"
Trump:	"Da."
Mueller:	"Is that a yes, Mr. Putin, I mean, Mr. President?"

A FIRESIDE CHAT

President Franklin Delano Roosevelt began a series of informal radio chats to the American public during a turbulent time in the 1930s. The radio back then was to communicating as Twitter is today. Here is an excerpt:

"My fellow Americans, it is whispered by some that only by abandoning our freedom, our ideals, our way of life, can we rebuild our defenses adequately, can we match the strength of the aggressors. ...I do not share these fears."

Trump demands a quaint, televised, fireside chat to compete with FDR. Here is a sneak preview:

"My friends, Hillary Clinton will never see the inside of the White House again as long as I live.

"You people love me so much that I know you want to keep me as your president for life. The Constitution now allows this extended appointment of the executive branch. Our blessed homeland needs me to lead it. I have authorized *The Enabling Act*, borrowed from German Chancellor Adolf Hitler's proposal to restrict powers of the Reichstag in 1933. His SS troops made legislators give up their civil liberties and transfer state powers to the Reich government. I'm pleased to tell you that the Democrats will sign away their legislative powers while my ICE agents surround the House of Representatives. I have the power to dissolve Congress and allow my Cabinet to pass much needed laws to *Make America Great Again*. And I pledge to you that all fake impeachment activity to convict me has ended.

"My first act tomorrow will be to have House Speaker Nancy Pelosi and Shiftless Adam Schiff picked up for questioning to ascertain their patriotism for the United States.

"I know I've been accused of a *quid pro quo* with Ukraine. There is nothing wrong with finding the truth about liars and cheats like Slow Joe Biden. And there's nothing wrong asking a nation to help with uncovering wrongdoing by a corrupt man. As your President for Life, I will always tell you the truth. When I make a promise to you, I keep it.

"This concludes the first of my fireside chats. I can't wait to tell you what I have in store for other scum Trump haters."

WAS IT A GOOD WEEK FOR TRUMP? AH . . . NO

The Week of February 16, 2018

1. The immigration DACA program reaches a stalemate and collapses.

2. A mass shooting in a Florida high school leaves Trump pondering what to say and do.

3. Porn star Stormy Daniels says she received a $130,000 hush money payment from Trump's attorney for sex with a spanking thrown in. A rolled up copy of Forbes magazine with a photo of Trump and his kids on the cover is used as a paddle.

4. Environmental Protection Agency Secretary Scott Pruitt is cited for wasteful first-class travel expenses.

5. Veterans Administration Secretary David Shulkin is found hiding paperwork that allowed his wife to travel to Europe on vacation at taxpayers' expense.

6. Mueller has indicted 13 Russians for interfering in the 2016 presidential election with Trump team collaboration. The week has not ended. It's only Friday at noon.

7. Update Friday 2:05 p.m.: Trump reportedly had a nine-month

sexual affair in 2006 with 1998 Playboy Playmate of the Year, Karen McDougal. She was paid $150,000 by The Enquirer for her exclusive story as a buyout fee – called a "capture and kill"— to keep the story hidden from the press. We still have Saturday and Sunday to get through.

8. Update Sunday Evening: It's just been reported by The Los Angeles Times that Rick Gates, a former campaign aide to Trump, has agreed to plead guilty and serve 18 months in prison in exchange for testifying against Paul Manafort.

ANOTHER EARLY MORNING CHAT WITH BOBO

Trump paces around his private living room in the presidential quarters. It's 3 a.m., so Bobo begins to tweet. Trump's only remaining trusted friend tries to calm him down.

Trump: "Bobo, they are all deserting me! My advisor Hope Hicks is leaving me. Her assistant is also on his way out. My trusted assistant Rob Porte was forced to resign. My attorney general won't fire Mueller. My chief economic advisor Gary Cohen is about to resign if I impose a 25 percent tariff on steel and aluminum. What am I gonna do? Morale in the West Wing needs to grow like the stock market."

Bobo: "At least you have Ivanka and Jared, your trusted daughter and son-in-law around."

Trump: "Jared has failed to get top secret security clearance. I need him to…well maybe I should just get rid of everyone."

Bobo: "Cheeses weepers, Donny, why don't you put me in charge of something instead of having me just tweeting? I can pass an FBI top security review, Donny! No one has anything bad to say about me. And I know a lot about international stuff, at least I know as much as you-know-who, ahem, Kushner."

Trump: "Bobo, I might do that! I trust your advice completely. I could get rid of Kelly Conway and make you chief of staff. And I need a new attorney general. So if I fired Jeff Sessions and put you in charge, would you fire Mueller? You're right, I need a clown in office. Lots of 'em. The ones I hired are not listening to me."

Bobo: "OK, I'll be chief of staff."

Trump: "We'll see Bobo . . . maybe."

Even Hope (Hicks) has left the White House.

REX TILLERSON IS FIRED AND A BUNCH MORE STUFF

March 17, 2018

Rex Tillerson, secretary of state, was fired. When the under-secretary of state for public affairs, Steve Goldstein, later in the day spoke about Tillerson being uninformed about his firing, he too was fired.

On the same day, Trump's personal assistant, John Mcentee, was suddenly escorted off the grounds after Homeland Security discovered he had committed serious financial crimes.

Last year, Tillerson called his boss, the President "a moron." Even though the description is true, it didn't add to his job security.

When Trump hired Mike Pompeo to be the new Secretary of State, his old job as CIA director was filled by Gina Haspel, deputy director of the CIA and resident dominatrix. Haspel ran a detention center in Thailand back when torture was trending in 2002. She water boarded prisoners and had their heads slammed into walls.

All of these events took place on Monday. Let's see what fortune brings by the end of this week.

Update March 17: Assistant FBI Director Andrew McCabe is fired just days before retirement thereby losing his retirement benefits. An all-out war ensued between Trump and the FBI. If Sessions had not fired McCabe, then Trump would have had grounds to fire Sessions and appoint another attorney general who would act on orders of Trump to fire Mueller, which would have ended the pending subpoenas, accusations, testimonies, convictions and prison for a whole bunch of people.

It's just another week in Washington under Richard Milhous Nixon – I mean, Donald John Trump.

IT'S A DARK AND STORMY NIGHT

April 10, 2018

The White House staff has long since gone home. A cold, early spring wind howls. The old hallway cuckoo clock strikes midnight as Trump slumbers with Bobo the Clown, his one remaining buddy. The rooms and halls are eerily quiet. Even the normally hyperactive Bobo is quiet as he senses something is amiss.

Trump: "Bobo, no one likes me anymore. They don't like people who know everything."

Bobo: "But I still like you, Donny. You'll always be my president, no matter what. You're my best friend, Donny."

Trump: "When I went to Saudi Arabia, my other best friend, King Salman bin Abdulaziz, said being king was more fun than being president. And I agree with him. Bobo, did you hear that? There is a noise in the Lincoln Sitting Room. Let's go check."

Ghost: "Ohhhhhhh Donald? Donald J. Trump, first King of the United States. Do you know who this is?"

Trump: "Bobo, it sounds like . . ."

Nixon: "That's right, Sir Lancelot, it's your old Richard 'Slippery Dick' Nixon – number 37, a ghost, at your service. I spent my last days in office getting drunk in this room talking to Henry Kissinger. I was hysterical, you know, just like you are now. I cried. My enemies were growing just like yours. The cover-up will getcha every time. You know something else, Trump, expanding a war zone or starting a new one won't distract people from these problems you've caused. I tried that already. And you know what else? They don't have Dick Nixon to kick around anymore, now they have you! Hoo hoo hoo!

"Hahahahahahahahaha."

Trump: "Did you hear that, Bobo, the ghost of Richard Nixon howling through time?"

Bobo: "I heard it, too, Donny. Should I tweet this spooky stuff about Nixon? You always let me tweet in the morning."

Trump: "No Bobo, just go to the kitchen and get me a bottle of Scotch."

Bobo: "But Donny, you don't drink."

Trump: "Watch me Bobo. Watch me. I'm gonna get plastered."

BEAM ME UP, SCOTTY: SCOTT PRUITT'S *"NEW AGENCY FOR HOLISTIC STANDARDS THROUGH UNOBSTRUCTED POLLUTION"*

Formerly the Environmental Protection Agency
April 13, 2018

If anyone gets into trouble in the Trump administration, just wait a few days until someone else gets into more trouble! A new disaster always comes waltzing in to take center stage and nudge out the current intolerable mess. Trump hops from one fiasco to another so the firing of Environmental Protection Agency Administrator Scott Pruitt will not be a matter of concern for long.

Syrian bombing missions take the limelight off excessive personal spending habits of EPA director Scott Pruitt.

The Trump EPA has painfully become a dysfunctional shell of what it was. Science and research have been sidelined and global warming is called a figment of wild imagination. The already minuscule budget has been slashed by 30 percent, making enforcement actions impossible. Superfund enforcement (requiring polluters to clean up their toxic spills) has been reduced to the current interest rate.

The new EPA lost 700 employees. The House Appropriations Committee approved $31 million for Voluntary Early Retirement Authority (VERA) and Voluntary Separation Incentive Payments (VSIP) to buy out contracts of existing staff. Now the polluters are running the show. A mining operation in Alaska's Bristol Bay goes forward after being blocked. One oil leak could destroy the largest sockeye salmon resources in the world. No more banning toxic pesticides and no more requirements for companies to disclose hazardous chemical inventories.

Welcome the return of smog, bigger and more profitable *Trump Smog* – coal ash, mining waste, benzene and mercury pollution. Get your oxygen tank and face masks out. Invest in air purifiers and carbon filters.

It's profit at any cost. Fossil fuel is Trump's renewable energy. Dirty energy industry lobbyists and CEOs are the new guards at the American power and utility gates.

"He's a fantastic person. I just left coal and energy country. They love Pruitt. They feel very strongly about Pruitt, and they love Pruitt," Trump gloats.

Normally, this kind of accolade is a prelude to being fired. But normalcy doesn't thrive in this Trumpian era. Scott Pruitt resigned for using government funds on himself and his wife.

May God bless his little-soundproof-Chick-Fil-A-wifey-used-Trump-Hotel-mattress-cheap-rent-condo heart.

ENVIRONMENTAL PROTECTION AGENCY

"Hello, EPA, may I help you?"

"This is Shelby Connor from Parrish, Alabama. We've had 260 box car loads of dog gone shit sittin' at our rail yard for months. It stinks."

"That's a state matter. Did you call the Alabama Department of Environmental Management?"

"What ya'll mean? These trainloads of shit have come down from New York. It's a federal inter-sate matter."

"Sir, please be respectful. It's human waste."

"I don't care what you call it. It's stinkin' up our town. We can't even go to a Little League baseball game 'cause the boxcars are right across the tracks. How would you like to drive to church on Sunday and take a whiff of it while praying to the Lord?"

"Did Trump send this stench down here because we didn't elect Roy Moore? Let me speak with your director."

"Sir, Mr. Pruitt isn't available. And he no longer reviews environmental issues. Our new mandate from the president is to help companies get rid of waste the cheapest way possible. They probably picked Alabama because your dumping rates are so low. You'll have to call the West Virginia office to file a complaint. They handle waste disposal. Oh wait, that office has been closed down, too."

"I wanna know why New York and New Jersey's shit is sittin' in our little town. Git the stuff outta here."

"Shelby, shouting into the phone won't get you anywhere. I'm trying to help. Here, let me give you the Denver office. They have experience handling bio solids. Oops, sorry, that office was recently closed, too. Mr. Connor, we're not going to be around much longer as an agency. The EPA is shutting down. Haven't you heard?"

"I voted for Donald Trump. And now he's turning his backside on us."

"The president is doing a great job getting rid of regulations so more jobs can be created. Do you know how many people you could employ shoveling that sludge into a dump? Your residents could have more work for generations. I suggest that you could turn this waste into fertilizer-rich compost and grow organic vegetables."

"You got a point there. That's why we voted for him. I need a second job, too. How can we git more New York bio waste?"

TRUMP MEETS KIM JONG-UN

May 2, 2018

The host, President Moon Jae-in of South Korea: "Mr. Trump, please may I introduce you to Marshall of the Democratic People's Republic of Korea, First Chairman of the National Defense Commission, First Secretary of the Worker's Party, Chairman of the Party's Central Military Commission, Standing Member of the Presidium of the Party's Political Bureau and Supreme Commander of the Korean People's Army, Kim Jong-un."

"You mean Little Rocket Man?"

"Mr. Kim Jong-un, may I introduce to you the most perfect inspirational American thought-leader, The Commander-in-Chief, President Donald J Trump."

"You mean the American Dotard?"

The American Agenda:

1. All nuclear bombs must be removed from North Korea.

2. Infrastructure technology to construct weapons must be destroyed.

3. A UN international team will remain a permanent watchdog agency to oversee nuclear activity.

4. All scientists who have worked on the nuclear weapons pro-

gram of the Democratic Republic of North Korea will be fed to hungry dogs.

Kim: "Ah Trump, I have much experience feeding my uncle to hungry dogs. I even perfected disposing of my half-brother in Malaysia using poison with the hanky-rubbed-in-the-face method. After our scientists are eaten alive, we cook the dogs and have a banquet of tasty American hot dogs for the loyal people of North Korea?"

Trump: "President Kim, you could be very useful helping me get rid of my fake news enemies. For one, my chief of staff keeps calling me an idiot. The list keeps growing. Mueller is numero uno to be fed to your hungry dogs. Lock-her-up Hillary would be a sight to watch as she tries to shimmy up a tree as one of your hungry dogs pulls her down.

"Kim, if you promise to bring some of those dogs to Washington to unleash on my enemies, I will sign a peace treaty with you."

Kim: "Will that include a State dinner, Mr. Trump?"

Trump: "Complete with hot dogs and cheeseburgers on the grill."

TRUMP GOES TO BED WITH A CHEESEBURGER

July 27, 2018

Through another leak in the White House, it's been established that instead of returning to the bed chambers with his wife at the end of another difficult day ruining America, Trump goes to bed with a double cheeseburger. Cheeseburgers can't talk back and even more so, because there is no need for him to explain to a cheeseburger the frustrating reality that after years of using Propecia, he can't achieve a presidential erection (or election.) And it's anyone's guess what insults Melania might sling at her husband, if she were around.

No, a cheeseburger is the safe way to go. His wife reportedly sleeps in another room.

While munching his cheeseburger, he ends a disturbing day by wondering if his former friend and attorney, Michael 'Mr. Fix-it' Cohen, remembered the conversations and meetings with Russians in pursuit of compromising information on Hillary Clinton. Cohen remembered a whole lot more since charges were pending against him. That's old news. Cohen went to prison. Then he was released but later, went back to prison for violating terms of release, and now released again, presumably to write his own book.

Since Trump's son Donald Jr. lied to a Senate hearing about his father not knowing about the meeting with the Russians which was then contradicted by Mr. Fix-it, he could face a perjury charge. As Daddy Trump pondered the probability of a prison sentence for his son, might he fear resigning the presidency in exchange for clemency? Or let his son go to prison.

Giuliani claimed that Cohen lied. "I expected something like this from Cohen. He's been lying all week. He's been lying for years." The Washington Post's fact-checking blog claims that Trump too, has lied many thousands of times since being in office and before.

The only remaining pleasure that Trump has is going to bed with a cheeseburger.

MOE, LARRY, CURLY AND RUDY

May 18, 2018

Which one of these fellas is a member of the Trump administration?

Answer: All except Rudy Giuliani; he is the new legal guy in the White House hired to clean things up, after spending years as mayor cleaning up the sex parlors and peep shows in New York.

Giuliani has long been associated with closing down the seedy joints on 42nd Street and its environs. Maybe that's where he met Trump. Now as the legal liaison to a promiscuous President, Giuliani is sure flip-flopping on morality and ethics.

No more pay-to-play street sex. Not when his boss pays for sex in five-star hotels. Giuliani starts damage control by saying that Trump did in fact pay off Stormy Daniels to remain silent. But then the president admonishes Giuliani for not having his "facts straight." "Virtually everything said has been said incorrectly, and it's been said wrong, or it's been covered wrong by the press."

Now, Giuliani refers to the transfer of hush money as a "nuisance payment."

"I never thought $130,000 was a real payment," said Giuliani.

So will Giuliani go after illegal immigration, as he did in 1994?

"Some of the hardest-working and most productive people in this city are undocumented aliens. If you come here and you work hard and you happen to be in an undocumented status, you're one of the people we want in this city. You're somebody we want to protect . . . " Oops. Not anymore.

Instead of dressing in drag for a function in New York, Giuliani now dresses up as a clown and joins Larry, Curly, Moe and Bobo in the Trump administration.

TRUMP IS CLEAN AS A TOILET HANDLE

July 15, 2018

Trump pleaded with Russia during the 2016 election to hack the campaign records and emails of Hillary Clinton. On July 27, 2016, he cried:

"Russia, if you're listening, I hope you're able to find the 30,000 missing emails."

On July 15, 2018, the dictator Putin and wannabe dictator Trump sat down for a summit in Helsinki, Finland. No scribes were allowed in the room, but someone has now revealed the conversation.

And so it came to pass that Russia hacked the accounts of Hillary Clinton and democratic operatives. Both Trump and Russia were amply rewarded for this act of treachery. Trump became the first president in history elected by a Russian dictator. And Russia, the longtime enemy of Western democratic tradition, became a new investment partner and mentor to tired old Uncle Sam, who lords over a disquieted tribe of manic-depressive, freedom-loving, patriotic simpletons formerly known as Americans.

Trump: "Vlad, thank you for helping me with the new Trump Moscow Hotel. Everyone thinks that we are exchanging international secrets!"

Putin: "Donald, you dog, you know how to throw them off pony trail. In Moscow, we have Russian mafia to pay off. They demand special favors."

Trump:	"It will be a tremendous hotel, unlike anything seen before. Ok Vlad, let's go to the press conference and talk about dismantling NATO. No one will ever guess what this meeting was really about. We're gonna make a lot of money on it."
Trump:	"Oh, and Vlad, is that old shower scandal forgotten?"
Putin:	"Da."
Trump:	"Good, it was pissing me off."

ANOTHER PRESS CONFERENCE

November 13, 2018

Trump: Ummm... excuse me. I I don't know Matt Whitaker, my new attorney general. He's a very respected man. I never heard of him. Hell, I don't even know the woman who stays upstairs on the second floor... what's her name, Melania?

White House Reporters: Mr. President... Mr. President... Mr. President...

CNN Correspondent Jim Acosta: Mr. President, the special prosecutor Robert Mueller has finished the investigation into Russia's interference in the 2016 election.

Trump: Here we go again. You're a rude, terrible person. The way you treat Sarah Huckabee Sanders is horrible. That's enough. Put down the mic. You should be ashamed of yourself. CNN should be ashamed. It's a fake question.

NBC's Peter Alexander: In Jim's defense, he's a diligent reporter who busts his butt like the rest of us.

Trump: Well, I'm not a big fan of yours either.

(Acosta begins talking without a mic)

When you report fake news, which CNN does a lot, then you are the enemy of the people.

Helen Thomas: Mr. President, why do you really want to go to war?

Trump: What the hell are you doing here, Helen? You're dead. How did you get in? You're a ghost. Get out of here.

Helen Thomas: No, Mr. President. We reporters never die. We will stalk you forever. Ghosts don't need credentials.

GEORGE HERBERT WALKER BUSH'S LETTER TO INCOMING PRESIDENT

January 20, 1993

Dear Bill,

When I walked into this office just now I felt the same sense of wonder and respect that I felt four years ago. I know you will feel that, too.

I wish you great happiness here. I never felt the loneliness some presidents have described.

There will be very tough times, made even more difficult by criticism you may not think is fair. I'm not a very good one to give advice but just don't let the critics discourage you or push you off course.

You will be our President when you read this note. I wish you well. I wish your family well.

Your success now is our country's success. I am rooting hard for you.

Good luck — George

(Trump's future letter to the incoming president in case he manages to stay in office for the full term)

To Whom it May Concern,

When I first walked into this office just now I felt the same sense of disappointment that I felt four years ago. The place was smaller than I am accustomed to at Mar-a-Lago. And it was rundown from the previous tenant.

Time has passed by all too quickly. But I finally got my wall built from the Gulf of Mexico to the Pacific Ocean. No more illegal *pendejos* sneaking in. And I've made America great again! The Covid did a great job of reducing Medicare and Medicaid payments.

I wish you great happiness here if you can do some side deals for me, Joe. I felt the loneliness of being without a real wife. My childhood friend, Bobo, has been a great companion helping me compose so many important Tweets.

There will be very tough times, made even more difficult by criticism you know is fair. I'm very good at giving advice. Never let critics discourage you or win any debate about the environment or human rights. Screw them all.

You will be our president when you read this note. I hope you don't prosecute me. There is nothing to discover. I wish your family well.

Your success is completely my success. I'm rooting hard for you to push the new Trump Hotel complex being designed for the front lawn of the White House.

Good Luck.

Donald

ANOTHER 'TRICK-OR-TREAT' AT THE WHITE HOUSE

Presidents like tradition and ritual
October 28, 2018

For the second year in a row, Trump and Melania opened the White House gates to Trick or Treaters. The president has dressed as Hitler and Melania is dressed as his lover, Eva Braun. Visitors are required to go through full-body pat-downs and all guests must pass through a scanner. Electrified barbed wire surrounds the perimeter of the White House where guests pass over a lagoon stocked with alligators. Prison spotlights shine on the path leading to the North Portico. German Shepherd dogs growl as an enhanced security measure.

Trump: Melania, what did the staff buy for giveaways this year? Is the candy made in the USA? We gotta employ Americans.

Melania: Donny, I tought you vanted to save money. I told dem to buy cheap candy from China.

Trump: NO, not China. New tariffs have been implemented which includes candy. What the hell?? Let's get this thing over with.

(Pointing at a guest)

Hey, who are you dressed as? Are you a ghost or goblin? Maybe you are . . . Brett Kavanaugh. Is that you, Brett?

Kavanaugh: I don't want any candy. I already ate too many sour grapes. I want beer, lots of beer.

Trump: Melania, you handle but don't get too close. No? Ok, let's move along. Look, there's a bunch of kids waving flags but not the American one. Is it the caravan from those shithole nations? What do you kids want? We don't have any pinatas. Take some Hershcy Kisses, now go march over to that waiting bus with bars on the windows. *Adios pendejos.* Next?

(Pointing at a zombie)

You sound like . . . John Kelly? This night is for kids to spook each other, not me! Not me. Melania, give him some Snicker Bars. Next?

	Hey, you have a Kanye West mask on. Is that you, my soul brother?
West:	I love you and you are *Making America Great Again*. Just don't call me a you-know-what tonight. Gimme some M&M's, man.
Trump:	Take all the M&M's you want. Wow, here comes a real ghoul. This one is really beginning to scare me. He's headless. He looks like Jamal Khashoggi. Where is your head, Jamal? Melania, give him some Butterfingers. That'll teach you to mess with my Prince of Darkness. I have a hotel planned for Riyadh.
Khashoggi:	Boo hoo hoo. . . .
(Next in line)	
Dracula:	Trick or Treat!
Trump:	No, you're at the wrong address. The undead party is across the street at Nancy Pelosi's house. Get outta here.
Melania:	Donny, the guest candy has all been given out. Let's go inside.

STATE OF THE UNION ADDRESS

January 18, 2019

Trump: Madame Speaker, Mr. Vice President, Members of Congress, First Lady of the United States, and my fellow Americans:

It's been a few years since I first stood at this podium, in this majestic chamber, to speak to the simpletons of this great land we call America—to exploit your fears, your aspirations, your nightmares, and your greed.

As your President leading you during this schmucked-up new year because of *The Nancy Pelosi Shutdown* of our government, and because I promised to protect you from hordes of Central Americans with a wall at our southern border with Mexico, I am celebrating by announcing a free Quarter Pounder at all McDonalds through the duration of the shutdown. I, your only leader, Donald J. Trump, will subsidize this Quarter Pounder with funds from Treasury.

When you apply for the free Donald Trump Quarter Pounder, include your name, email, phone number and address so I can send you promotional materials on re-electing me in 2020.

Over the last year, I have levied tariffs against China, so your appliances would cost more. I've withdrawn from that disastrous global warming treaty that President Obama foolishly signed. I've met with my new friend Kim Jung Un – a really great, fantastic man in spite of what they say about him starving and enslaving his citizens. They think he is a god – what could be better, right?

I have maintained our valuable alliance with our friends in Saudi Arabia through difficult times. My friend, Prince Mohammed bin Salman, has been implicated in the butchery of Jamal Khashoggi, just another fake news journalist. Congress will hereby give me the same powers to make critics like CNN correspondent Jim Acosta disappear and dissolve in acid.

I renew my promise to you tonight, the American people, that a wall of American steel, beautiful American steel, will be built along our southern border with Mexico. We will forge a new unity of spirit. We have seen the steel in America's spine. I call on all of us during this time of the shutdown of our government, to set aside our differences and to unite around my campaign promise to build our very own Great Wall of America.

With your guidance and Nancy Pelosi's obvious support, we will Make America Great Again!

A SWANKY SUITE IN A FIVE RED STAR HANOI HOTEL

February 28, 2019

Scene: President Trump and Supreme Commander of the People's Army of Korea Kim Jong Un, are in bed together eating popcorn and watching the public hearings on TV taking place in Washington D.C. Michael Cohen, the Trump fixer who said, "I would take a bullet for him," is testifying. and comes clean for all the sins he committed in defense of his former friend.

Supreme Commander

Kim: "Donny, pass the popcorn. This is getting interesting. If these hearings were going on about me back home, I would have the doors locked, than have hungry hyenas eat them all and show it live on North Korea TV. I could beam it to South Korea to show those dogs who the boss is on my peninsula."

Trump: "I'm likin' it, Kimmy Unni. More popcorn? Cohen is a rat fink."

Kim Jong Un: "Donny, what means 'rat fink'?"

Trump: "Italian mafia use it when someone betrays them. Then they hire a killer to get rid of him."

Kim Jong Un: "Donny, how can anyone call you a racist, a con man, and a cheat?"

Trump: "Unni, because I am! I'm proud of it, Kimmy."

(Trump and Un laugh, and laugh, and laugh.)

Trump: "Kim, I wish you could be my Vice President—love the way you control the people in your country. Gimme some more popcorn, Kimmy. Don't hog it.

"Kim, here are the papers to sign for our new Pyongyang Trump Hotel. Everyone thinks we had a summit to denuclearize Korea. Forgetaboutit. Keep the nukes. Let's make money. I will have a Trump Hotel in every capital city in the world. I love you Kim Jong Un. I really do."

Kim Jong Un: "And I love you too, Donny T. Want more popcorn?"

"NOBODY DISOBEYS MY ORDERS INCLUDING THE EASTER BUNNY"

April 18, 2019

Trump made this assertion while strolling around the Berchtesgaden in the mountains of Bavaria. Or was it on the South Lawn of the White House on an Easter egg roll with the Easter Bunny? Or was it in response to insinuations in the Mueller report that aides routinely defied his commands?

The Easter Bunny was partaking in the Easter egg roll when Trump's security advisor, Stephen Miller, reported a possible security breach.

Miller: "Mr. President, I just received intel that the Easter Bunny was not born here, has no green card and no visa."

Trump: "Neither was my wife."

WHAT SOME ANCIENT RULERS HAVE IN COMMON WITH TRUMP

During ancient Egyptian dynasties, monarchs often defaced or destroyed statues representing the previous ruler to erase the reputation and deeds of the former ruler. Sometimes damage was limited to facial disfigurement as with Pharaoh Senwosrett III (1878-1840 BC) whose nose was broken off because ancients believed that the life force emanates through the nose.

Trump shares this goal when renegotiating and tearing up Clinton and Obama-era treaties.

NAFTA is one such remake that removes Clinton's name from the global trade agreement. As Politico writer Adam Behsudi quotes Lori Wallace, director of Public Citizen's Global Trade Watch said, "For those who trusted Trump's pledge to make NAFTA 'much better' for working people, it's a punch in the face because the proposal describes TPP (Trans-Pacific Partnership) or any other same-old, same-old trade deal." There are no improvements — only the removal of the Obama legacy and any other former president's name.

This symbolic effigy-smashing of Obama extends to the Iran Nuclear Deal, to recertify to Congress every 90 days that the Iranians are complying with the rules; the Paris Climate Agreement; The Affordable Healthcare Act and all other agreements that Obama successfully negotiated regarding the environment and human rights.

In the land that I call home, tens of millions of Americans who couldn't tell the difference between shit and Shinola, resulting in the election of a malevolent quasi-life form that makes George W. seem like Jesus, Moses, and George Washington rolled into one. Maybe our next president, if we are still electing presidents that is, will take cues from Trump and the ancients as well. A good start would be remove any future White House portait of him that might eventually be installed.

MOCKUMENTARY MINI SERIES

Italian movie director Federico Fellini III, grandson of the master surrealist film director of the same name, has been hired to direct this soon-to-be American classic.

Casting: Wendy Williams will play Omarosa as the evil, conniving, tape-recording messenger from hell. Kevin Spacey will play Rudy Giuliani and Giuliani will be a set consultant now that his main client is out of office.

Rosie O'Donnell will play Sarah Huckabee Sanders and Asia Argento will play Kellyanne Conway. Attorney General Jeff Sessions will play himself as will former FBI Director Michael Comey. Trump will be played by a large, foul-smelling pile of batshit.

Scene 1: A meeting of the Trump family at Trump Tower before the historic election. Omarosa's tape recorder has been hidden between her boobs to gather information for a future tell-all book.

A Russian attorney Natalia Veselnitskaya, hands over Hillary Clinton's emails. Her boss in Moscow, Vladimir Putin, sips vodka while watching a 2013 video of a naked Trump during his infamous stay in the presidential suite at the Moscow Ritz Carlton Hotel in 2013 while the Miss Universe pageant aires.

The main character, Trump, has been a learned pile of batshit for so long the stench no longer negatively affects those who work for him. He decides to assume human form and run for president and concludes his administration will help market more Trump hotels.

WHY ARE WE SCREAMING AT EACH OTHER?

The answer to this question is how we elect our political leaders. Most members of Congress are owned and paid for by special interests, working both sides of the aisle depending on which business or institutional clients they represent. There is no concern for the health and stability of our nation: the focus is only on creating laws to increase profits for their clients and shareholders. The country is a capitalist corporation business vying for profits, not services.

Patriotism is the opiate for the masses to calm the exploited population. We the People are damned. The unmitigated influence of money is a rarity in other democracies. A British journalist lamented about our health care system and asked, "Why don't you Americans rise up in rage and change things?" Because we have been divided, beaten and conquered. How can one fix anything including gun control laws when money always wins and laws are purchased by the highest bidder?

In 2002, Senator John McCain sponsored and passed the McCain/Feingold bill limiting soft money influencing elections. But then the trusty ole conservative majority of the Supreme Court, who purport to support individual rights (until it restricts the super wealthy from gobbling up more wealth), decided that political spending was a form of free speech in *Citizens United v. the Federal Elections Commission* in 2010. This court created new ways of corrupting the political process.

Trump is simply the personification of government gone wrong because money has become the only decider. No principles, ideology. No ethics. And now we have a near dysfunctional, dystopian society in the Land of the Free and the Home of the Brave. The blue collar worker now fears having a reduced income or no income at all. This worker seeks to augment his income with a part-time job to make-up for the middle income wage he once earned. As his puppet strings are yanked, he pulls the lever (the wrong voting lever) that opens the trapdoor on which he stands with a rope around his gullet.

TESTIMONIALS AGAINST JOE BIDEN

Leaked by Unnamed White House Sources

"Joe Biden introduced me to cannibalism when I was President. Most Americans are unfamiliar with this proclivity of his, but he does enjoy a tasty roast of human leg around the holidays."
—*Idi Amin, former President of Uganda for Life*

"Biden once groped me in the hallway of the Capital after coming to Washington on a bus trip with my class."
—*Unnamed High School Student*

"Joe Biden sold crack cocaine to my mother and pleasured himself in front of my father."—*Former White House Intern*

"Our new leader is Abu Ibrahim al-Hashimi Joehami al-Biden."
—*Islamic State Spokesperson*

FALLING INTO THE WRONG ARMS

The country had a relatively stable eight years under Barack Obama, not perfect but there was economic growth. However the aftermath of the Bush wars opened the doors of hell and the laws of unintended consequences dominated.

And it came to pass that as a new election neared in 2016, a creature walked to the stage to suspend reality and make enough voters believe that he would lead the nation to wealth and weapons for all.

Cajoled by this socially mangled, misanthrope who has perfected the fine art of the lie, bigotry and unfair tax relief for the wealthy, they naively followed this most foul leader off the cliff.

Wait. What am I doing here? Am I trying to present a logical reason why someone would not vote for Trump? That's totally insane. That's almost as insane as voting for Trump! Plus, having to go through all that socio-economic, psychological, and historical crapola is about as interesting as a Xarelto commercial. So, I'm going to reveal the cause of the disease that I am dubbing, "Trump Voterism" or simply, "TV": a vicious parasite, mutated by toxins now allowed into our air, water and food by Trump's relentless attempt to kill all of us by loosening our environmental regulations.

Not only does that explain the phenomenon, it also sets the stage for an entirely new series of blockbuster movies, all based around these parasitic mutants. Think *The Purge* meets *Invasion of the Body Snatchers* meets *Citizen Kane* meets *Tremors*.

There, can we move on to examining why people do other stupid things, like falling off a cliff while taking a selfie?

TROUBLE IN THE WEE HOURS

In the East room of the White House

"Where is Bobo? Bobo, where are you?"

"I'm here, Donny, hiding behind a curtain."

"Why, Bobo? You don't have to hide. I'm always here to support you. Screw critics. I didn't say that Sessions was a 'dumb Southerner,' I said he's a 'dumb fricken Southerner.' I'll take this God-damn bottle and…"

"No Donny, don't throw your golf club at George Washington's portrait! Oh my God, Donny, I'm your friend. Calm down. I'll make you a cheeseburger, a double cheeseburger, Donny. Just the way you like it with fried onions."

"I want to know WHO double-crossed me and leaked the Sessions remarks?"

"Donny, staff took your executive orders right off your desk."

"How do you know, Bobo? Was it you? Are you *Deep Throat*? Did you write that disgusting New York Times Op-Ed? It was you, wasn't it?"

"Donny, I have a few friends for you to see this morning. There are 25 of them from your cabinet."

(*Bobo pauses and states with newfound authority…*)

"General John Kelly, please come in."

(*And with that, the Trump cabinet marches marching into the East Room*)

Bobo: "Donny, you are being relieved from the Office of President. I was sworn into office this morning. You will address me now as 'President Bobo.' I will pardon you so you can return to Trump Towers and continue making money full time and so I hope we can still be friends."

"You mother fricken' piece of petrified wood. I'll have you burned, Bobo. No one's gonna believe I'm being replaced by a clown."

LADIES AND GENTLEMEN, THE 46TH PRESIDENT OF THE UNITED STATES

September 7, 2018

"My fellow Americans, I declare that we are finally free from the yoke of my former mentor, Donald Trump. With a heavy heart, I decree that the witch-hunting fake news demigod of an administration is dead. Today you are all free-ranging American Bobos.

"I was sworn into office in the bunker of the White House basement, the same bunker where my predecessor hid when the protestors converged in Lafayette Park across the street. I will serve the remaining term of our former president. My first important duty will be to distribute a t-shirt with an image of me on the front and the slogan on the back saying, "Making Crazytown Great Again 'MCGA'." We will source it through Ivanka Trump's Chinese producers, and create a tariff exclusion for this special import. These t-shirts will prove that a new day has dawned.

"My new Vice President is Stormy Daniels.

"Our nation needs time to heal and put our troubled past behind us. Vice President Daniels is throwing a party on the White House lawn and the public is invited. She is rehearsing a new dance for the party."

A COUP D'ÉTAT TO MAKE AMERICA GREAT AGAIN

My Letter to a Friend and his Return Letter

"Dennis, I'm gonna draw up a petition tonight that calls on the American military through the Joint Chiefs of Staff, to suspend the Constitution until Jan. 20, 2021 when a new president will be sworn into office. The military will immediately escort Trump off the grounds of the White House and place him in home confinement at Mar-a-Lago.

"The military will install a junta; a six person team representing the Marines, Air Force, Army and Navy, Coast Guard and now, the Space Force. Elections will proceed as scheduled but without Trump leading the Republican Party.

Are you ready to sign it, Dennis? Are you ready to take a stand for your family, community, state and nation?"

"You must be reading my mind, Bill. I've been saying this for weeks. I will sign it in a heartbeat. The Thief-in-Chief must go before he kills all of us. He is the biggest mass murderer in American history, bar none, and the toll climbs every day. The murderous slimebags on FOX should also be included in this purge, since they are equally complicit in this.

And, since there are still so many who don't mind dying for Trump, I would also strongly encourage red state Trump toadies to mass gather at churches, bars, whatever, and drool, spit, and ooze bodily fluids on each other, and then wait in line for ventilator treatment that could have been avoided if they had only listened to Dr. Fauci before catching COVID-19.

It looks like we just fixed the country. Now, what about McConnell and those other grinning jackals?"

Signed: Dennis Kaplan

THIS CONVENTION OF CRIMINALS AND CLOWNS

Ruinous tax cuts, destructive tariffs, white supremacy, devastating trade wars, political bullying, modern-day concentration camps, attempting to buy Greenland, attempting to sell Puerto Rico, asking the Israeli PM to ban two American congresswomen from visiting Israel, misusing government funding for personal gain, denying climate change and making the EPA a shell of itself. What can we do now?

Vote! These absurd adventures of Trump and our collective nightmares will only end after two months and a few weeks from November 3 when Trump is not elected for a second term.

Much damage will continue. The global pandemic will not end until a vaccine is discovered and distributed. Trump has abdicated his responsibility of protecting the people and now we are experiencing tens of thousands of needless deaths. Trump is by any definition, a mass murderer with his neglectful response to the pandemic.

By criticizing our allies and befriending our enemies, Trump is a traitor in the White House — forking over secret intelligence to the Russians. He is not a wise man. His pathological dishonesty and thousands of false or misleading claims have turned truth into a game of lies and deceit. He is a menace. When he was elected, we didn't expect our worst nightmares to come true. May we all survive this catastrophic episode in our nation's history.

Trump has hurled hatred and insults at everyone, like the paper towels he threw in Puerto Rico at desperate, homeless residents after a devastating hurricane. And we are, like those homeless refugees, desperate to grab paper towels and wash our hands of this total failure of Trump as a person and president.

IS IT OVER?

Reagan: "Government is not the solution to our problem, government IS the problem." When a second rate actor became a second rate president, he set the stage for reality TV hoaxes to become our government. Distrust in government, in my time, began with the Vietnam War. Does it end now with the death of thousands of our most vulnerable citizens from Covid-19? Does it end with a deranged leader at the helm? Does this ship sink?

Like *Noah's Ark* in Genesis or in older variations in Mesopotamian culture, or later iterations found in the Quran, appearing as *Safina Nuh*, we now wait for these rains to end and for a new beginning.

It's not over. But first, the rains must end.

And we must VOTE Trump out of office.

SYMBOLIC PATRICIDE OF DON JUNIOR: "TRUMP HAS THE CHARISMA OF A MORTICIAN"

"Trump has the charisma of a mortician, and the energy that makes Jeb Bush look like an Olympian." May 25, 2023

This was spoken by Don Trump Jr. on his online Rumble platform, "Triggered with Don Jr." and the name Triggered happens to be part of the title to his book, "Triggered: How the Left Thrives on Hate and Wants to Silence Us." My book was originally titled, "It's a Lie, It's Fake News, It's a Total Political Witch Hunt." But Raymond, a friend of mine, suggested Donald's Vanity Tantrums." I'm sure glad I listened to him. It's short and to the point unlike Don Jr's.

Maybe Don Jr. made a faux pax because he seems to be really rooting for his dad. And perhaps he just got confused since he had been discussing Ron DeSantis' run for president. Right before his infamous line, he conjectured that, "…Ron wants people to think that he's like, 'Trump-lite' or something like that. He's not, either on policy grounds or personality." (Another emerging Trump family intellectual? Fear not — no.)

Or maybe, just maybe, Don Junior harbors a deep-seated resentment of his ole man for among other things, once slapping the shit out of him when he attended the University of Pennsylvania's Wharton School of Business as daddy Trump knocked on his dorm door to take him to a baseball game. His son wore a Yankee jersey as he opened the door. A roommate of Don, Scott Melker described that "…his father slapped him across the face, knocking him to the floor in front of all his classmates." He made his son put on a blazer and tie.

There are plenty of examples of the son's revenge against his father and patricide is found in history and mythology and maybe Don wanted to finally subliminally vindicate himself with a verbal rumble against papa. One example of patricide that comes to mind is Oedipus, a king of Thebes who killed his father and married his mother and in my humble opinion, this Trump family kind of action wouldn't be unreasonable given what we now know about them.

Here are a few other interesting examples of patricide that might equal the symbolic doing-in of Trump by Don Jr. Kashyapa I of Sri Lanka around 473 CE killed his father King Dhatusena by sealing him inside a wall.

Crown Prince Dipendra of Nepal massacred most of his family at a party in 2001 before shooting himself in the head. That kind of action would make a toasty ending to a Shakespearean Mar-a-Lago affair. Who knows, maybe Don Junior continues to harbor resentment for his father slapping the shit out of him that day at Wharton School of Business.

THE WOMEN'S MARCH ON WASHINGTON JANUARY 21, 2017

It just seems like yesterday

I am traveling to Washington DC this Saturday to participate in the Women's March on Washington. I am going because the threat of President Trump to defund Planned Parenthood. I don't need any other reasons to show my solidarity. There is no need to augment my decision with the realization that Mr. Trump has no morals or business ethics; which insures that he will make a horrible leader.

I am somewhat surprised that the overwhelming majority of marchers are in fact, women. But hey, it's a "Women's March" right? The evening before the trip, I listened to commentators on the PBS Nightly News that a "massive March is being planned." During the table discussion, someone asks if only women are going. Another commentator answers "…and other hangers-on." That's me, the hanger-on. I have always been a hanger-on so this is not news to me.

I have anticipated the nuances of being in the middle of a huge throng of marchers. I packed four eggplant Parmesan sandwiches (made the day before) and two bottles of water. I took Imodium tablets a few hours before leaving on buses reserved for this event. I can't predict my bowel movements at my age anymore and it wouldn't be wise to get stuck in a crowd of a million women with sudden bodily needs. Ahem…

A Hartford Courant reporter sits next to me. Of all the women travelers on board, I get the chance encounter to sit next to a guy. I anticipated sitting next to a woman so I could elicit her perspective on the March.

Our four buses depart from Trinity College in Hartford and we all arrive at RFK Stadium later this morning. Most of us decide to walk the two miles to the Mall. It's a historic and ironically festive occasion. Many avenues are filled with joyful marchers as we converge near the Capital Building.

I cannot get close to the stage area. I'm now stuck in the crowd unable to move. The marchers that are close enough to the stage can hear speeches. The rest of us automatically cheer when a speaker makes a good point and this cheering is like a water wave that sweeps over the ocean of humanity. A yell is heard from the masses and it's probably Madonna screaming something about wanting to blow up the White House (as this was later reported in the press). I slowly squish myself through sliver of openings of the throng until I reach some scaffolding remaining from the inaugural the day before when Mr. Trump was sworn to uphold the laws of the land.

I reach the scaffolding and look up at climbers scurrying through the monkey bars. I pause a moment and consider my sixty three year-old bones. I pause only for one moment. Now I too have joined the club climbing up the bars. Sixty is the new forty and I know I can make it up to the top. Besides, I need my panorama photos of the crowd.

My photographic studies are done. I have climbed to the mountain top (of the scaffolding). It nears two PM, the time at which my Connecticut Congressional delegation has opened their office reception room nearby at the Sam Rayburn Office Building for us marchers to rest, use the lavatory and enjoy a light lunch. They are kind and generous to offer this accommodation for their constituents. Congresswoman Elizabeth Esty thanks us repeatedly for making the trip. The room is quickly filled with fellow marchers sitting at tables and on the floor. We soon clean out the food. After the much needed rest, it is time to slowly walk back toward the Stadium.

This event evokes past marches to Washington DC especially President Nixon's anti-Vietnam protests of the 1970s. And the big anti-Vietnam march of 1967 when as a child of 14, I boarded the overnight Amtrak train. My experiences have taught me that a march doesn't change anything. But an accumulation of marches and grass-roots organizing can and does change the body politic. President Trump will have his day in the sun. I haven't the slightest doubt that it will be for one term only. But a person can do a lot of damage in four years.

An announcement is made at the reception that the march through the streets has been officially canceled because of the crowd size.

On the return bus ride home, we make a rest stop in New Jersey. I need to use the men's room. But the men's room this moment is no longer for men only. It's been co-opted by hundreds of women returning from Washington. Why not? There are maybe nine women to every one man waiting in a long line at the entrance.

And now, I am waiting to go. One woman turns to me and says, "Oh, you don't need to wait. The urinals are available." I guess she thought I only needed to go pee pee. She was correct. But as I began to enter the lavatory, a voice in me said that this was an historic moment - of sorts. I yell out, "this is a fucken photo opp" as I yank out my IPad. I shoot those waiting in line. I enter the facility and continue shooting. I sense that I need to shoot quickly and get the hell out before a disgruntled male takes an issue with my camera. Before I have finished with a few different photo perspectives, a man yells something at me and at that moment, I exit.

It's interview time. I have turned my IPad to video and say something to the effect that, "This is a unisex bathroom now. We're not in North Carolina - it's New Jersey. This is the new era of Trump." I try to get the crowd in a jovial mood. And as I yap on about the ancient Roman men and women using the same go-to rooms, I swivel my camera and ask others standing in line about the practical need to share the same lavatory.

I'm back on the bus and a much needed sleep.

MY CAT BABE AND DONALD TRUMP HAVE SOMETHING IN COMMON

April 5, 2023

Recently, I prepared to have a spaghetti dinner but I couldn't find the bowl that I normally use. I looked high and low for the bowl. I walked through every room in my house searching for it. I opened every kitchen cabinet. I even went into the basement on the off chance that I decided to eat my pasta in my unfinished basement. No bowl. Could I have put the bowl somewhere during a sleep walking episode? I never thought I had a sleep walking problem but one shouldn't rule out any such possibilities. Nothing. The bowl was gone. Then, as I sat back in my studio with my feet up on my desk, I looked up at a shelf and there was the bowl. After eating my pasta one evening, I had placed it there a week ago so one of my cats couldn't get at the remaining tomato sauce and olive oil. Babe has a voracious appetite and he will eat anything he can get his paws on. And if he had gotten hold of my pasta dish, he would have had another diarrhea episode around the house. And cat diarrhea is no fun to wipe up.

This all reminds me of the need to keep private citizen Donald Trump away from the White House least he again, crap all over the institution as he did the first go 'round. He was so unfit and unstable that certain military chiefs had to insure he couldn't get his hands on the nuclear codes during his last days in office. Those who were and are his supporters conveniently forget these moments. But I will never forget how much Trump crapped all over America.

Every word out of his mouth was a lie. He befriended our enemies and made life difficult for our friends. He hired the worst creeps into administrative positions. He likely gave up national secrets to Putin. He encouraged an insurrection when he didn't get his way to be re-elected. He deregulated as much as possible and in case you forget, regulations are put in place to protect its citizens. He stole multiple boxes of confidential documents and not only refused to give them up, but had them piled in a bathroom and a performance space and had more scattered on floors. He reduced taxes for the wealthy corporate community and now that we have runaway debt, the republicans are doing a blame game on the democrats. Par for the course.

Let's not forget that Trump has something in common with my cat, Babe, who was found almost newborn and deprived of food in my driveway on a cold December morning a few years ago. He's a wonderful cat now. But if he gets anywhere near some remaining oil in the frying pan or anywhere near my pasta bowl, he will lick it up until he splats diarrhea all over the floors of my house — just like Trump will do if he is re-elected by those who think he has their best interests at heart.

By the way, he doesn't have our interests at heart. He has no heart. A narcissistic personality disorder reveals that truth.

FRED JACKSON AND THE SECOND AMERICAN REVOLUTION

(Homage to Donald Trump's 'Proud Boys' and Others)

Fred Jackson was a proud rebel in The Great Northern Militia Alliance. He and his wife Ruth were often found hosting summer neighborhood barbecues. They easily found new supporters for the coming war to take back America. Fred stationed himself at the pit and handed out chicken legs drenched in homemade sauce to new, unsuspecting recruits — kinda like a politician on election-day would do; promising a chicken in every pot. Talk of big government, guns and revolt would come later.

Fred and his cohorts believed themselves to be the direct Anglo-Saxon descendants of America's 18th century rabble-rousers who tossed bales of tea into Boston harbor after news of the British Stamp Act reached these shores. But tea-toddlers, they weren't.

He was proud of his new-found abilities to recruit and had recently been promoted by the Alliance to the rank of sergeant of his own local militia. Wasting no time consolidating resources, Fred collected everything from boxes of canned food to crates of assault weapons. All were discreetly stored away in basements and underground bunkers in his local neighborhood.

Strategic plans were soon underway as this historic moment arrived, the moment to take back America. A secret, unnamed Northern

Alliance militia representative from high up the chain of command visited one evening to give a short pep talk to the men and their wives in the basement of Jackson's home.

"Ladies and gentlemen," the mysterious commander said, "the time has come to act. We must stop the tyranny and treasonous actions of our government. Today we take action. We will starve the beast into submission. We will bring the entire nation to a screeching halt by whatever means are necessary. And we will un-steal the election. You know who I'm talking about; the great populist himself, codenamed, "OrangeFatso.""

"Yep"… they screamed in unison, "Save our leader, OrangeFatso."

He jabbered on like this awhile longer and then said something about how it was one's duty to avoid payment of taxes like they did in the Boston revolt.

A rebel in the audience was overheard mumbling that, "Maybe them damned liberals wouldn't be so bad if we could just shoot a few." as he cleaned and oiled his weapon. After the rousing speech ended, the mysterious speaker made way out of Fred's hatchway as quickly as he had arrived and was driven off into the night before anyone could ask questions.

The next day, Fred called for another drill. The basement was a good place to train without attracting attention. His supportive wife listened from upstairs as she tapped her foot to the muffled sounds of her husband's marching orders.

"Left…right…left…right…left…right…left…right."

During the drill, Fred's wife heard her husband cry,

"Oh no… not again. I told you not to march forward in the cellar."

"Ruthie honey," Fred yelled from the basement, "Billy bumped into the wall again and now has a nose bleed. Quick, get me an ice pack."

One thing that should be noted about the division of labor between the men folk and their women; it was written in the Northern Militia Alliance's "Code of Conduct" that men would do the fighting and the women would play supportive roles – just like in the olden days of the founders. Their women were as important as Betsy Ross – who is thought to have sewn the first flag – was to the cause of revolt.

The country of Fred's birth was no longer recognizable to him. Waves of foreigners had migrated across the unprotected southern frontier. His leader had often spoken of building a really high wall to keep out the hordes. The government, Fred believed, was overrun with big-spending liberals and nanny-state socialists. Fred even thought that his own past president of the United States was born in another country.

"He wasn't born here. You know he owes his allegiance to the United Nations," cried Fred.

Encrypted communiques were now being sent and received with increasing frequency throughout the "Alliance." The days of waiting had drawn to a close.

And so it came to pass. The militia teams began assembling. They gathered along every mountain pass and byway. They took positions beside bridges and waterways. Fred's platoon prepared to assault its assigned mountain. This really was only a big hill but these rebels had a tendency to magnify everything around them including the importance of their mission. Their watches were synchronized.

Sergeant Jackson finally gave the order to charge.

"CHARRRRRRGE!" he screamed.

The men began their long, wild, rickety-split charge to the top of the assigned hill. Fred held his assault rifle in the air with one hand, and with the other grabbed his pants before they slipped down below his protruding belly – an unfortunate victim of too many beer-drinking strategy sessions.

Well they whooped and hollered for so long that soon most of the militia troops were out of breath. By the time they reached the summit, the sergeant could be heard cussin' (at no one in particular.) He wondered if he had rushed up the wrong hill. His GPS repeated, "recalculating... recalculating..." His phone vibrated on his belt and he quickly grabbed it and listened intently.

His head turned slowly downward as he stared at his mud-caked boots. His heart was pounding. He was breathing fast.

"Yes sir, I see. But when are we...? Win the hearts and minds, first? But...OK, I'll inform the men."

The sergeant ordered roll call and sadly told his men that not only did they seize the wrong hill, but the unseen generals had decreed that this was only a drill. The real revolution was yet to come but now, without the element of surprise. Dejected, they began to hobble down the green hill.

Then suddenly, Sergeant Jackson received another message. This time, he could hardly contain himself. Something new had just happened and word was spreading like wildfire. His fingers quivered as he responded:

"I'll tell the men right away." The sergeant rallied the now exhausted rag-tag men around him and excitedly yelled,

"All hands to Burns, Oregon. The government is assaulting some ranchers. The Bunkerville boys from Nevada are leading the counter assault. I'll be driving out at first light if anyone needs a ride."

Fred finally made it home in his Ford pick-up truck while still sweating from the long charge. His dear sweet Ruthie waited at the half-opened door as dusk settled in.

"Come in my hero. I made your favorite hot soup for you."

Fred stumbled in and sat at their kitchen table and slurped down the refreshing food. He then went straight to bed without explaining anything to his worried wife about the disappointing details of the false deployment.

Fred dreamed about the new revolution soon to sweep the land of his birth – the land he hardly recognized any more. And he dreamed that his name would one day be enshrined 100 years from now, along the nearby interstate highway where he lived. The sign would read: "The Sergeant Fred Jackson Expressway: Named for a Patriot of The Second American Revolution Who Stood His Ground and Helped Take Back America."

Then Fred farted and repositioned his head on the pillow as he slept like a baby all night long.

THE CITIZEN KANE MOVIE OF TOMORROW: CITIZEN TRUMP

February 17, 2024

The classic movie *Citizen Kane* directed, produced, and starred in by Orson Welles will one day in the future, have a remake only this time the main pseudo-fictional character will be Donald Trump. The movie scene will open with a very bloated relic of his former self; uneven orange-smeared makeup slobbed across his face in bed. His overgrown blond hair is found similar to the muss of Boris Johnson's now showing gray roots from lack of up-to-date hair dye. He periodically wakes from a semi-conscious state at his future dilapidated Mar-a-Lago residence (for lack of having sufficient funds to upkeep the property due to previous constant litigation and losses.) He looks around demanding more Kentucky Fried Chicken wings as low paid service personnel rush in another bucket and his last word is not "Rosebud" as in the movie Citizen Kane but:

"Stormy." And the ex 45th president of the United States expires. The camera fades to black then opens at Le Club in the early disco 1970s, a members-only Manhattan nightclub in the East 50s, where models, fashionistas and a variety of Eurotrash (including his wife) went to be seen.

"The government has just filed suit against our company," said Trump, "saying we discriminated against Blacks. What do you think we should do?"

The Roy Cohn obedient ass-kisser to Senator Joe McCarthy hearings accusing entertainment personalities of being communists shoots back, "Tell them to go to hell and fight the thing in court and let them prove you discriminated against them."

Roy Cohn has become Trump's go-to lawyer and fixer.

Cohn admonishes the young Trump to 1. Never settle. Never surrender. 2. Counter-attack, counter-sue immediately. 3. No matter what happens, no matter how deep into the shit you get, claim victory and never admit defeat.

These lessons were found to be the essential attributes of his future self.

And so it was.

THE DONALD CONFESSES HIS SINS

May 5, 2025

"Bless me Father, for I have sinned. It's been 300 years since my last confession. I've lied. I've cheated all my life and I've swindled everyone I've ever met in my life. I once grabbed the you know what of our Virgin Mary but she was made of stone and she didn't feel a thing. I've never told the truth and that's the truth so I just now lied again. I've cheated the government out of its fair collection of taxes and I've fabricated real estate transactions to show a loss when there were gains. I even once founded Trump University just to swindle unsuspecting young and naïve kids probably the same ones who I convinced to vote for me because I'm the greatest President of the United States even greater than George … what's his name. I filed bankruptcies over and over again and that was quite a crock of shit.

My one-time mentor from way back, a really good man by the name of Roy Cohen, groomed me to, "1. Never settle and never surrender. 2. Counter-attack and counter-sue immediately. 3. No matter what happens, no matter how deep into the shit you get, claim victory and never admit defeat." And you know Father, Roy Cohen was right. Everyone should have a Roy Cohen in their lives.

I love this country so much that I'm starting a new dance craze called, "The Goose-Step Two-Step March." "You link arms on the dance floor. As you move backward in line, you turn you head to the right and lift your left leg straight up as far as it will go. Then you step forward and turn your head to the left and lift your right leg up. It's very similar to square dancing and pretty soon the floor will be filled with goose-steppers. Forward, backward round and round. If you step out of line, the caller will detain you, interrogate you, strip search you, and send you off to detainment camps where airplanes will be waiting to send you off to the paradise of Central America, San Salvador.

Most recently, my AI device on Truth Social placed my image in the papal garments of yes, your next Pope.

Father, if you can convince some cardinals to vote for me as your next Papa in the Vatican in Roma, I'll nominate you to be a cardinal as well. And that's a promise I will keep, as usual.

Dominus vobiscum, Father."

FROM THE OFFICE OF TRUTH SOCIAL: DONALD TRUMP

A Once Great Nation

June 9, 2025

"A once GREAT NATION, far and above any other nations on earth, is now inhabited by a disgusting, fat-farting, lying, second-rate pretend mafia hood with a nice color-toned hair piece in the fabulous but small inconsequential White House; I'm referring to myself, of course and all the disgusting hanger's on I've appointed that don't know squat about the positions that I appointed them to.

I have consulted with my architects that I have yet to pay from the last job they did for me at Trump Tower to study tearing down this shabby White House and replacing it with a carved marble structure honoring me as your leader for all time. There will be sculptures of your humble servant gazing out at the four corners of the universe."

(Trump is everything evil. There is not one decent bone in his body. He is pure evil and 100% destructive. If there were such an animal as an antichrist, he would be it. My only question is, why did he have to live in my time?)

THE FRICKEN DISASTER WHICH IS TRUMP AND PROJECT 2025

June 25, 2025

Trump and Project 2025 is doing incalculable damage to the United States. How does one rebuild the international aid we so generously developed over time since President Kennedy established the agency in 1961. Giving aid to the less fortunate is no longer a priority since the savings can be directed to the super wealthy. He is attempting and rather successfully, to destroy our international student studies programs at various universities that incubate the brightest of young minds and who often stay here and develop new technologies businesses. We were the first among nations. Trump wants it destroyed probably because he was never intelligent enough to understand the value of bringing the brightest minds to America. International scientists working on all manner of new inventions are beginning to realize they can't survive here in the US since federal grants are being terminated all so more wealth can be diverted into fewer hands in the Big Beautiful Bill. They have destroyed the EPA which has protected the people from industrial harm.

The administration has declared war on immigration. Our system has been broken for many years. This inability to fix immigration is no doubt due to our electioneering which is now controlled by humongous dark money courtesy of the John Roberts Court in 'Citizens United verses Federal Election Commission' which recognized corporations as people and hence, opened the floodgates of corporate financing of elections. No nation on earth allows open borders yet the Biden administration did not act forcefully enough during the first two years. Why couldn't he foresee this being an important issue to Americans? I'm in favor of controlled immigration. Both of my grandparents originated in Europe. Now ICE agents are no more than Gestapo-like federal thugs hiding under facial masks to drag people off the streets similar to nationalist movements and here I'm thinking of the Nazis in Hitler Germany. Today I'm likely hiring a contractor group (a man and two women from south of the border) to repair aluminum siding on my house. I don't care whether they are undocumented or not. They know their business and they have quoted me a fair price. I don't want them to be deported. They are valuable members of our community. I will offer them refuge in my home if they need sanctuary by the time they finish.

THE MEDIUM IS THE MESSAGE

A Marshall McLuhan theoretical study made in 1964
June 29, 2025

As I walked the streets as a hippie in 1967, a new pop phrase was added to our lexicon; 'The Medium is the Message.' It was coined by Canadian communication theorist Marshall McLuhan in 1964. In my fuzzy world at that time, I wondered what it signified. Did it mean that the message wasn't as important as the medium in which it was communicated? Well, I never got that far until I read a study on how the far right media has swamped their messages 24/7 on every conceivable medium.

Perhaps 20 years ago as I ran for exercise down my street into Cedar Hill Cemetery in Hartford to continue my run through the peaceful hilly burial grounds, a small stone and granite company existed across the street from the cemetery gate. The building is attached to a house. The owner frequently sat outside beside his business with his AM radio blaring Rush Limbaugh's radio program. I found it irritating to listen to it as I ran past. I thought the business owner hadn't much better things to do like cutting gravestones then listening to a foul-mouth Limbaugh spout diatribes on whatever democratic side political issues were being ridiculed. And I thought as I ran, "Who the fuck could fall for that obvious crap? Who?"

I now have my answer. Anyone who self-selects an extremely one-sided menu of commentary all day long can fall for it. Donald Trump is the net end user and victor of this 24/7 propaganda. The Hungarian authoritarian leader Viktor Orban said that control of the media through consolidation, media buyouts, or shutting down media is the path to successful autocratic rule. He is, by the way, a dear friend of you know who.

It's no longer truth in media that is important in this 1984 dystopian environment. Social media plays an equal role. The Haitians in Springfield, Ohio eating cats and dogs rumor began on Facebook. It persisted long enough that Fox and a host of other media picked up on it. Then in the presidential debate, Trump confidently (with a big CON) stated in a matter of fact that "They're eating cats and dogs." to which Kamala Harris let out a huge spontaneous laugh. Preposterous right? Funny? She made me laugh. She made anyone laugh that was aware that it was all made up. But the other side knew what they were doing. Junk, garbage, lies, it doesn't matter. Say it repeatedly and it will be believed. Joseph Goebbels, propaganda minster under Adolf Hitler, knew the importance of repetition. The far right media was sowing the seeds of doubt; of disinformation. Our little cell devises were grooming whole generations of listeners and readers 24/7.

This media expansion was carefully choreographed over decades. Rush Limbaugh finally died but not before being given the Presidential Medal of Freedom award in 2020. This is how low we have sunk as a people.

"THEY'RE EATING CATS AND DOGS SAYS J.D. VANCE"

Here is a little song I wrote. It's on YouTube: https://www.youtube.com/watch?v=BiNusL05JUo (And please listen to my other compositions on YouTube @Catman Bill. Thank you.) Enjoy the music. It's the only thing I can do to add my voice to the resistance besides writing this book.

In Springfield they're eating dogs
And now they're eating cats
What can a childless Catman do
With those erroneous facts
Maybe move to Katmandu
Or flee in a catamaran
Or just move to Katmandu
With my girl and dogs and cats

He broke down the doorways
Of the Capital
They followed his directives
So tyrannical

In Springfield they're eating dogs
And now they're eating cats
What can a childless Catman do
With those erroneous facts

Maybe move to Katmandu
Or flee in a catamaran
Or just move to Katmandu
With my girl and dogs and cats

THE EMPEROR HAS NO CLOTHES

July 19, 2025

The emperor has no clothes. And what is being revealed metaphorically is the shit bag tittered to his leg being used for drainage of a lifetime of lies and false promises. The golden question now that the fog is lifting and MAGets are dispersing like cockroaches from a flashlight, will he choose the easy way out via suicide or spend the brief remaining moments in his castle hoarding ill-gotten wealth with constant demands for bucket after bucket of Kentucky Fried Chicken.

Now after 6 months and then, three and one half more years of destruction of this once imperfect democracy, he plays with our world like a child in a sandbox. Although he is only the figurehead backed by the insidious Project 2025 which is of course a carefully thought out road map for the total destruction of our way of life. This poison that has manifested in our body politic for so long from the innocent days of Nixon (and before) through Reagan's anti government slander to the Gingrich and Bush era destruction now culminating in the final act. It's no wonder and how predictive Ben Franklin's admonishment to the woman passing by the Constitution Convention asking what did they get (from the convention) to which he allegedly replied, "A republic if you can keep it."

Even Rome burned.

My daily life consists of trying to buy local as much as possible.

Staying away from factory foods filled with sweeteners that fatten one so we need to eat and buy more to satiate our ever growing appetites and bellies. Then take expensive diet pills to lose weight. I now have developed a taste for black coffee with no additives. I'm frugal; I'm not a materialist (but I could be) and don't surround myself with such. I reuse things. I even dump the vacuum cleaner bag out and reuse that as well. And no I'm not cheap I just don't have any need to buy what others tell me I'm supposed to buy. I drive an old Toyota van because it's only going to get smashed anyway (distracted driving is par for the course) and it has already encountered a fender bender last year. I donate to good causes and one new one is public television because of Trump's desire to control the media through defunding independent journalism and direct increasing wealth to the super wealthy. I serve nature and the environment as much as I can.

As despairing as I sound, I sense that the inevitability of the pendulum will shortly begin shifting back to some sense of decency.

"…Excuse me, while I kiss the sky." Jimmie Hendrix

GHISLAINE MAXWELL: "TRUMP TOLD ME NOT TO BRING HIM ANY GIRLS OLDER THAN 14"

July 23, 2025

The Justice Department sent a legal team to the Federal Correctional Center in Tallahassee, Florida and Maxwell blurted out that, "Trump told me not to bring him any girls older than 14." Before she could say anymore on the record, legal staff ran from the prison and raced back to the airport. Deputy Attorney General Todd Blanche immediately called House Speaker Mike Johnson and advised him to cancel holding any hearings and cancel the pending subpoena for Ghislaine Maxwell.

"Mike, do not bring Maxwell to Washington. She is a lying wench and her testimony will permanently turn waring MAGA factions against each other. Maxwell just told me President Trump is a pedophile.

"Have the president call Pete Hegseth and order another bombing of Iran. Or anywhere. Send a few B-52s to Cuba that autta take everyone's mind off the girls."

(Or maybe Miss Maxwell is lying her brains out insisting The Donald had nothing to do molesting women as a get out of jail ticket. Just maybe.)

THE NIGHTMARE THAT HAS BECOME REALITY

August 3, 2025

I was certain that everything that is occurring under the current administration would happen again as it did in the first go-around. But Round I was childhood training wheels for the 2nd run. Most people or at least, a very large segment of the American population unfortunately have short memories. Donald Trump proved to be the modern Antichrist by 2020 yet we voted for him again.

      I believe that many people revenge vote, which means that if you don't like what the current president is doing, you cast your vote for the other candidate but this time the other is the one true Antichrist. He knows only destruction and self-aggrandizement. I would liken such figures in our time to Adolf Hitler, Benito Mussolini, Pol Pot, indeed even Benjamin Netanyahu fits this description for killing more than 50,000 and starving 2 million victims by Israeli government oppression of Palestinians who have lived on their lands for hundreds and thousands of years. And this just so he can keep out of prison and stay in power. While Trump has not killed yet in concentration camps, his behavior has led to hundreds of thousands needlessly dying in nursing homes in 2020. His vile hatred inspires his followers to kill indiscriminately. Certainly his closure of many agencies of government that protect people here and abroad will ultimately lead to premature deaths.

Why did so many Americans revenge vote? Certainly the missteps (literally) of Joe Biden cannot be dismissed. I have no need to regurgitate it. But to turn away from the stability of government and revenge vote is unconscionable. One must too, consider our online cell devices that have changed human behavior to be more aggressive; having shortened attention spans - a device that separates us into aloneness instead of bringing us together (as Zuckerberg once stated) and makes us prone to political grooming. The world community walks around with cell devices because, well, they can. And the tendency is to converse with the person in front of you unless or until the cell gives notice of an incoming message. Does anyone realize how fucking irritating it is to stop mid-sentence just so the person you are communicating with can measure instantly how important you are against the next incoming call and that call usually supersedes you unless you have money on the table.

In a "Star Trek: The Next Generation" segment from "The Game" in 1991, the "Starship Enterprise" is infected with a hand-held computer game that leaves the user addicted to the games as they exhibit orgasm-like responses to the game wins. And the business of interstellar exploration is badly affected. Does that ring any bells? How far-sighted of the writers to project this hand-held device as the potential ruination of Starship America. This device arguably contributed to a massive socialization crisis and turned many voters to kiss off American Democracy by electing the AntiChrist of our time.

STATE'S RIGHTS: STOPPING DEPLOYMENT OF FEDERAL TROOPS

August 30, 2025

A few months back I spoke with a few State Capital police officers in Hartford, Connecticut and asked if they would protect residents from jack-booted thugs of ICE kidnapping and was told they could not on account of it being a federal matter. That was then this is now. It's most certainly time for blue state governors to have a dialogue with their senior national guard commanders as a first step to protecting residents of each state. These governors must also interact with each other as a strong single voice as they prepare to meet with the military beginning with the Joint Chiefs of Staff on down. The reason it's so important to initiate this protective state response now is to end future pending consideration of military invasions. And the media must be included in a big way. California was already invaded as well as Washington, DC. The administration is already on record to consider invading Chicago and New York and other cities.

Donald Trump will not stop at dismembering all federal government agencies that protect the health and safety of its citizens and causing as much destruction as he is allowed. His sole purpose is to channel as much wealth into the fewest hands possible.

There is history of states having sovereign rights that the central government cannot and must not violate. The revolutionary war was fought over the oppression of a central authority. The British crown was the first central authority for which the war of independence was fought. Today, we are in a historic struggle to return our representative republic which is eroding at this very moment. It's tragic that we cannot even depend on the arch-conservative Supreme Court to protect "We, the People."

The sooner we in blue states demand an end to military interventions in our individual states the more likely we will succeed. If Trump's legions develop a taste for future state invasions, it likely will be done. The irony of support for state's rights was historically mostly argued favorably in Republican-ruled states until now.

And lastly, please come out to rally repeatedly for our freedom. Most state capitals and many cities and towns will be fighting to take back our nation. And please write, call, and email your governor asking them to move forward this idea that I have expressed. Now is the time. Not tomorrow.

Peace to all of us.

One August day as I drove home from Tennessee along I-81 in Pennsylvania, a phrase kept going around in my head "There's good people and bad ones wherever you go. Just seems like the bad ones are stealing the show." Songwriters know that if you don't write down lyrics when that mysterious Devine inspiration visits, it's lost forever. I quickly pulled into a truck stop and wrote it down and I had my composition within the week. An early version can be found on my YouTube channel under "Catman Bill - Hartford." Enjoy.

BLUE DAZE

By Catman Bill
August 10, 2019

I like the sunshine everyday
Even like the rains of early May
Cold winds are fine on a winter's day
I want it all to stay this way

One thing I don't like and you could guess
The ass in the White House making a mess

There's good people and bad ones wherever you go
Just seems like the bad ones are stealing the show
They twist and shout make others scream
Their deeds are causing a horrible swing

I like the sunshine everyday
Even like the rains of early May
Cold winds are fine on a winter's day
I want it all to stay this way

You've been sold I high priced bill of goods
He'll turn all your friends into mean ugly hoods
He'll say he's done nothing wrong at all
Than put you in detention halls

One thing I don't like and you could guess
The ass in the White House making a mess

I like the sunshine everyday
Even like the rains of early May
Cold winds are fine on a winter's day
I want it all to stay this way

A Trump sandwich is made out of white bread
It's full of baloney and a Russian spread
Day and night it's what we are fed
He tweets and he feeds as more lay dead

I like the sunshine everyday
Even like the rains of early May
Cold winds are fine on a winter's day
I want it all to stay this way
I want it all to stay this way

TRAGEDY AT THE WHITE HOUSE

(It's Being Reported...)

August 27, 2025

It's just now being reported that Elon Musk and his son were in the Oval Office this morning and his son reached into his snout again pulling out a booger and this time wiped it off on President Trump's designer suit jacket. This sent Mr. Trump into a rage as he ran from the office through White House hallways and up into the presidential living quarters where he dashed into the presidential bathtub and sank like a stone and drowned.

A hastily assembled press meeting was called and Press Secretary Karoline Leavitt announced through her cracking voice that the president had expired. And no more details were given except that a funeral was being planned for Labor Day Weekend. A jackass-drawn caisson will transport the president from the White House to the Capital where he will lay in state for several months in an open casket until an Egyptian-style sarcophagus that's now being planned (using sought after Carrara marble from Tuscany) is completed next to the Washington Monument.

More details at noon.

JAMES COMEY, HILLARY CLINTON AND I NEED A DOUBLE SHOT OF WHISKEY

September 26, 2025

"It's Deja vu all over again" said Yogi Berra. And so do I. I'm thinking that after January 20, 2017, the sun stopped rising in the east and the Wicked Witch of the West arrived to create chaos for all 4 years in office. Why would anyone believe otherwise. Why would anyone vote the same way as before? The answer is complex because humans are complex. We are a rational tribe one minute and the next minute we become irrational.

I was doing a bit of stand-up at a Methodist church open-mic once and I was confident I would procure a bunch of laughs. They offer free meals to everyone and this was my pay. With the spirit of Mark Twain, I strode to the stage and announced to the congregation that God made a mistake allowing the wrong primates up the evolutionary trail. I proceeded to explain that the Bonobo primates which are found now only in the Democratic Republic of Congo, were the delegated bunch to walk the trail but Man grabbed the tickets from their hands and ran like hell.

Well, wouldn't you know, the Methodists didn't like my presentation. They behaved similarly to the Catholics, which I was one at least until 7th grade in Ole Saint Joseph Cathedral School in Hartford. The principal Father Emerling expelled me 2 weeks before summer vacation for refusing to get a butch haircut like his. It really wasn't so much the length of my hair. The nuns didn't like me. I was a troublemaker. I chewed gum in class. I was a little chatter box. And for those transgressions they put tape across my mouth and had me put my gum on top of my nose. And once I was sent to the janitor Mr. Macken so he could measure my head and he made cardboard donkey horns which I had to wear all day. They had finally found a way to get rid of me. They found my Achilles heel. I wasn't going to get a butch haircut at the beginning of the hippie summer of love in 1967. No way.

The Methodists didn't laugh at anything I annunciated that evening. I felt proud. And the next day I received a phone call from the pastor asking me to come in so he could explain how their congregation was a family-oriented crowd. I immediately apologized and told him it wouldn't happen again — but it did happen again and eventually they told me not to return. A month later I asked the host what was so wrong about my admonishment of God and she screamed, "Because God doesn't make mistakes." Now that was funny.

I have digressed now. And God did make a mistake. She let the shit bag into the White House again. Everyday during the first go around, Trump pooed on everything and everyone. Every day, every week every month. Did we learn? No because we frequently revenge vote when voting for a president. They will say, "The guy in office even fell asleep at the debate stage so let's vote for the one who once crapped all over the country."

The human race replaced a truly civilized group of Bonobos. They are a matriarchal group. The females have control and when the males begin acting up, the ladies restrict sexual contact and this calms the guys down straight away.

FBI Director James Comey did a J. Edgar Hoover on Hillary Clinton within days of the election in 2016 and announced that the FBI had opened a new investigation about the emails. Hillary lost. The world changed for the worst. The sun stopped rising in the east and the Wicked Witch of the West took over not once but a second time. This is so twisto that Trump is actually charging Comey with illegal release of the investigation that saved his ass at the last moment. And that's the truth, Ruth.

My friend Cynthia is doing promo for a local Whiskey festival tomorrow night in Bloomfield, CT and she has offered me a ticket. This time I'm going to drink - the good shit.

'TWAZ THE NIGHT BEFORE ... OPPSIE DAISY - WHAT WAS IT?

December 19, 2025

'Twaz the night or just a few nights before the Big One
When all through the house
Not a creature was stirring
Not even a mouse

I drank down some booze
A poor thing to do
But slept like a babe
In a manger would snooze

Went into a dream world without any clue
Of what was about to enter my view
A convoy of trucks and pay loaders too
Moved into place on South Ocean Avenue

Wrecking balls and cranes
Excavators as well
On count one steamed ahead
Demolishing all of Mar Lago views

From the road to the sea
Every manicured ground inch was plowed
Even the toilet room where once stacked
Government files were found
All were destroyed and pushed into the sea

I twitched and I turned
In my delirious state
Was I mentally confused
Had I wished against fate

It finally came true
All the floating debris
Still on the high seas
'Round it did float
To the Gulf of… Whatchamacallit
Mexico

FROM THE OFFICES OF THE GREENLAND NOBLE PEACE COMMITTEE:

January 20, 2026

"We, the Greenland Noble Peace Committee do hereby award the Noble Peace Prize to the most profound leader in the history of the United States of America. We recognize that Donald Poop Trump has brought stability and prosperity to egg price reductions and peace to Terra de Fuego for the meager fee of 40 billion dollars. This 100% carrot-gold likeness of Viking warrior Ivar the Boneless, son of Ragnar Lothbrok and cousin to Eric the Red and Thorkell the Tall, is granted forevermore to the greatest president of mankind. We welcome Donald P. Trump to our shores anytime for a cup of warm hemlock tea and good tidings."

ABOUT THE AUTHOR

Bill Katz didn't know what he wanted to become. His Italian-American mother sent him to St. Joe's Cathedral School in Hartford. The Sisters of Mercy were elated to have a student with a Jewish surname. At first they saw little Billy Katz as the biblical prophecy of Jewish conversion. That is, until he began to cause trouble and question authority. Eventually, Billy was expelled for refusing to get a haircut. At Hartford High School, Bill began writing satires for the school newspaper. Nixon provided Bill with material not unlike Trump has today. After incomplete studies at college, he purchased a one way ticket to Europe and backpacked around the continent for a few years, finally making Florence, Italy his temporary home. He returned with a new found interest in art and eventually became a dealer of African American art. Cat rescue is a constant interest. He is a singer/songwriter and he writes what has been described as "Songs of Conscience." If you search in YouTube, "Bill Katz, Hartford, Connecticut," you can listen to a few including "Blue Daze" and "Corona Pneumonia and the Boogie Woogie Flu."

www.ingramcontent.com/pod-product-compliance
Lightning Source LLC
Chambersburg PA
CBHW021106080526
44587CB00010B/400